The DAY the SUN ROSE in the WEST

Harold P. Clements

WESTBOW
PRESS®
A DIVISION OF THOMAS NELSON
& ZONDERVAN

WestBow Press books may be ordered through booksellers or by contacting:

WestBow Press
A Division of Thomas Nelson & Zondervan
1663 Liberty Drive
Bloomington, IN 47403
www.westbowpress.com
844-714-3454

Scripture taken from the New King James Version® Copyright © 1982 by Thomas Nelson. Used by permission. All rights reserved.

ISBN: 978-1-6642-0621-2 (sc)
ISBN: 978-1-6642-0620-5 (hc)
ISBN: 978-1-6642-0619-9 (e)

Library of Congress Control Number: 2020918199

Print information available on the last page.

WestBow Press rev. date: 10/13/2020

Acknowledgement Page

First off, thanks to my wife for her patience for all the time it has taken to put this book together. My special thanks to our granddaughter, Kalicia (Morrison) Clements, for the extreme time and effort she has given me. To Clare Ash Jr. for his help on the "Thrashing Day" chapter. Thanks to my son Sim Clements for capturing the cover and author photos. Finally, to whom this book is dedicated: our children, grandchildren, great-grandchildren, and to Jesus for His daily assistance in my and my family's lives.

Sim Clements Photography
Email: SimClementsPhotography@gmail.com

Introduction

Between my dad and I, we cover nearly 100 years of farming. Needless to say, the 20th century (the 1900s) probably had more changes than any other century since creation. I am attempting with this book to show the tremendous changes in those 100 years of farming which also leads to the edge of another area which talks about many other innovations. For instance, if I were to talk to my grandchildren or great-grandchildren and try to explain to them that in the early 1900s there was no electricity, no indoor plumbing, nothing like smartphones, internet, texting, video chats, social media, going to school via the computer, or going to the moon and back they would think I had totally lost it. Tie that phase of the book, in with the fact that we have been a singing family, singing God's praises now going into the fourth generation. Last but not least, I have described the many miracles in my wife's and my life which proves the power of prayer. We trust you'll enjoy, and God bless.

Contents

Chapter One
THE EARLY YEARS

My father was Paul S. Clements, born August 29, 1905, and died April 24, 1991, at 85 years of age; my mother Mildred L. (Royston) Clements, born May 29, 1910, and died March 8, 2002, at 91 years old. They were married on November 12, 1928. My oldest sister, Wilma L. was born November 8, 1930, and died September 22, 2017. I was born March 31, 1932, about sixteen months after Wilma, in the old HGB (Hayes Green Beach) hospital in Charlotte. I have two younger siblings, Darrell L. born on February 1, 1939, and my sister, Karen K. born May 8, 1950, both still living.

Although my dad Paul grew up on a farm, as a farmer and gardener, in the early years of their marriage they purchased a home in the 400 block of South Sheldon Street across from the Frobel school. The Frobel school was on the west side of the street and my parents' home was on the east side of the street. The old Seventh-day Adventist church was one place north of their place on South Sheldon, on the same side of the street.

Dad worked for the Charlotte Home Dairy, located on the west side of South Cochran in the same location as the Eaton Place restaurant is today. Dad mainly worked in the back of the store, freezing all flavors of ice cream, churning butter, candling eggs, and doing whatever else was necessary to prepare the food for selling in the front of the store. Dad worked six days a week, Monday-Saturday, twelve hours a day which is 72 hours a week, from 6 a.m. to 6 p.m. For the 72 hours, his take-home pay was less than $14. For extra income, dad raised vegetables, like squash, carrots, and other vegetables. For a reference point, he would raise, top, and wash a heaping bushel of carrots so there would be nearly a bushel-and-a-half for just 75 cents.

In those days, a customer could get ice cream cones, sundaes, shakes, and more. A single cone (bigger than two scoops would be today) was sold for only five cents and a double-decker (which was almost more than you could eat), sold for a whopping ten cents! My, how times have changed!

As a side note, there was also a Blue-Ribbon Dairy (later called the Creamery) owned by the Harold Root Family where my family brought such things as milk, cream, and eggs to sell. This Creamery was located on West Shepherd Street, right close to South Sheldon Street. On the south side of South Cochran Street, was the office of Dr. Lester Sevener, located between Home Dairy and Seminary Street, close to where the Eaton Federals Savings and Loans is located today. Other doctors were also in the building with Dr. Sevener's practice.

Before we leave the Charlotte area, I need to mention that my great-grandma Sarah Jane (Jenny) Stranton also lived on South Sheldon not too far from where my folks lived. It is interesting to note that the large two-story home my folks purchased was bought for $2,500. After leaving Charlotte, my parents moved to North Stine Road, which is about three-fourths mile from M-79 to the north. They moved to a tenant house owned by Mr. and Mrs. George Kline, which was located on the east side of the road. My grandparents, John and Glycine Clements, also lived on Stine Road, about one-quarter mile before the Kline's farm, but on the west side of the road.

The move to North Stine was probably early summer of 1935, and they lived there until January of 1938; then they moved and rented the Vomberg Farm of 120 acres for 5 and a half years between 1938 and 1943. While on North Stine, I started school in Kindergarten at the Millerberg school which was on the corner of Valley and Millerberg Road. Valley was about three-tenths of a mile further north on Stine Road. You turned right on Valley and the Millerberg school was one mile to the east on the northwest corner. That simply means Wilma and I had to walk a mile and three-tenths (of course, *both* uphill) to school. I started school in the fall of 1936.

In early spring of 1937, the teacher called on the kids, about twelve or fifteen of us, and said that there had been swearing words said on the school ground and she would be disciplining anyone caught using those words. I was called in two or three days later because a girl told the teacher I was swearing. I told her I was sure I didn't. She indicated that she didn't believe it either, but had to ask what I possibly said that made the girl think I swore. All I could think of is that it had been raining and my dad said it needed to stop so that we could prepare the soil for planting. While playing during the recess, the sun came out and just my natural response was, "Thank God the sun is shining!" Apparently, the girl considered that swearing. The school teacher just smiled and let me go.

Later that spring, my sister Wilma told me that mother had said that we could go to Bergman's to play after school. Of course, I was for that! And so, we went south on Millerberg Road one mile to M-79, turned west and went about three-quarters of a mile to the Bergman's, which was on the northside of the road. We had just started playing when the Bergman's phone rang. Understand this is the old crank type phone which was on a party line; each family had their own ring (two longs and a short, or whatever). Over the phone, my mother made clear that she never gave permission for us go and told Mrs. Bergman to send us immediately home and she would meet us. She met us alright with a fresh cut willow switch about 30 inches long. Now, remember when I was a kindergartener, though not fat, I was chubby and wore knickerbocker type pants. My sister was taller and skinner and frankly, at that time, was much faster. So, all the way home, I was the recipient of a very stingy willow switch because mother had no problem keeping up with me, but neither of us could keep up with my sister. I always reminded my sister that I took her punishment for lying, but in hindsight, I guess she was worth it.

My mother reminded us that lying was disobedience and there was a price to pay. I got the message. From Bergman's to the corner of Stine was about a quarter-mile and then three-quarter miles north to our home. I suppose you could say I received my sister's stripes but I guess in fairness when you consider that Jesus took the stripes for me, what I received was nothing.

In the early days (from 1920 to 1945 range), most homes had a cellar. This was usually located in one of two common places, the first at the back of the house with two large hinged wooden doors, with stairs that led to the basement, or the second access for many homes was from the backroom going down to the cellar so you wouldn't have to go outside. This underground area was intentionally kept dark. The reason for the "dark" room was to store winter supplies like potatoes, buttercup fall squash, and any other vegetables that you wanted to keep for a while.

Even after the homes got electricity, the owner would only use a small light bulb (like 15 watts) to intentionally keep it as dark as possible. When these were covered and below the frost line, a minimum of four to five feet from outside ground level, the vegetables would not freeze. It was not uncommon for farmers to keep a minimum of 10 to 15 bushels of potatoes in storage, along with all the other vegetables.

P.S. Just for fun, remember that he who throws dirt, loses ground! Ha.

Great Grandpa Paul Holding Baby Kristopher

Chapter Two

GRANDPA AND GRANDMA'S PLACE

My grandparents, John and Glycine, lived on North Stine Road, one-half mile north of M-79 on the west side of the road. They made their living over the years on just 40 acres, which would not seem possible in our day. The house of my grandpa and grandma was a two-story home in which they lived approximately 40 years. Interesting to note, at that time there was no electricity in the house or barn, so lanterns, candles, and flashlights were a standard commodity in homes of that era. For instance, the only way to pump water was to use a motor that burned kerosene to get water to the house and barn. The pump house was just back of the house between that and the barn. A very large cast-iron kettle was not more than ten feet back of the house, and it would hold about one hundred gallons of water. Grandpa would bring the horses out to water at the kettle, but he would also carry water to the barn as part of the evening chores. Grandma, of course, back in those days, didn't have any refrigerator but relied upon a small icebox to keep some of the items cool enough to last for a while.

The two-story house, had the needed backroom that all farms had, a kitchen, a large front room, a parlor, two downstairs bedrooms, and two upstairs bedrooms. The heat was provided by a large potbelly stove that was used for all winter heat and many times in the spring and fall. I should also note that there was a small porch on the south edge of the house with two doors, one in the kitchen, and one on the north end to the living room. The kitchen, of course, had a wood stove because of no electricity, so my grandma would have to get up early, get the stove het up (warmed), and ready for cooking, while Grandpa was doing the morning chores.

One very hot, humid, stormy day, when the doors were opened between the porch and living room, the front door going out to the road was also open (no air conditioning in those days!). There was a heavy bolt of lightning that generated an approximately 18-inch (in diameter) fireball that rolled slowly over the porch, through the living room, and out the front door! Although they were very scared, of course, they were told that it was probably a "cold" bolt because it never set fire to anything. I'm still amazed by this, but if Grandma and Grandpa said so, I'm sure it happened!

The drive from the road went straight into the garage, but also bent to the north between the house and barn, and right there was Grandpa's blacksmith shop. Grandpa's blacksmith shop had the old forge for heating iron, making horseshoes, or any other special adaptation that was needed for farming. Though the floor was dirt, it is hard to believe that my grandpa's blacksmith shop was so neat you would not be afraid to throw down a blanket and eat off the floor. However, as Grandma Donna would tell you, Grandpa John's neatness never rubbed off on me! Ha! Other buildings besides the barn, were the large tool shed, and a rabbit house where Grandpa raised rabbits. They were mostly of the white variety, some were sold as pets, others were, I hate to say, were sold for meat.

Both my grandparents were tenderhearted people. Let me explain. One day a car was coming quite fast down Stine Road to the north; just before you got to Grandpa and Grandma's place was a short steep drop in the road. A mother coon and her family were crossing and the car hit and killed the mother coon. Just like Grandpa, he gathered up the three baby coons and put them in the rabbit hutch until he could figure out what to do with them. For the record, coons are relatively clean animals, *if* they are given the chance. For instance, if there was water available, they would wash their food before they ate it. Back in those days, sugar cubes (about half-inch in size), were used for sweetening coffee or other items. To Grandpa's humorous side, he would give the baby coons a sugar cube and of course, they put it in the water to wash it and it would disappear. Now I know it's hard to believe, but the blank look on the face of those baby coons I can still see in memory's eye and laugh today.

Of course, we must mention that there was a little white house behind the big white house. Just imagine, if you were in one of these homes with no indoor bathrooms how you would hurry up your morning business in the winter months when you would have to dust three to five inches of snow off the seat before you sat down. Imagining doesn't even begin to do it justice. It was cold!

The large barn was two-stories, with the cow barn on the right side and the horse barn on the left side with a drive between. Above the cow and horse barns were the hay lofts that held the hay and straw for the winter months. Grandpa had not more than four or five cows to get milk, cream, butter, and the like. On the horse side, I believe Grandpa had three horses. His main horse was Duke, a large Belgium that weighed in excess of 2,000 pounds, with the other two horses being smaller and not as heavy as Duke. Grandpa was very protective of his horses, as you will see in one of my stories at the Vomberg farm, when he caught me abusing (in his opinion) the horses and gave me a lecture I didn't soon forget.

Grandpa's farm had tons of rocks on it to the immediate south of the buildings. There would be so many stones that you would have to take a flat stone boat, hauled by two horses, pick up stones and haul them to a stone pile. Shortly after World War II, tractors became bigger and stronger, caterpillar tractors would dig deep holes, push in the stones, and cover them with dirt, so farmers would no longer have to work around the stone piles to plant the crops.

Because of failing health, my grandpa and grandma (between 1946-1947), moved in with my parents on Carlisle Road, where they lived until Grandpa (John W. Clements) died February 1, 1955, at age 77, and Grandma (Glycine Evelyn Victoria J.) lived for several more years until her death on January 2, 1969, at 87 years. Our son Steven was born just a couple of weeks after Grandpa had died. Steven's middle name was John, named after both grandfathers: Grandpa Clements, and Reverend John I. Batdorff, who died September 6, 1955.

Grandma was always a huge help to my mother, partly because that was just normal for her, but she also had heavy arthritis in her hands and the hot dishwater made her hands feel much better. So, you better get out of Grandma's way when she was going to do dishes. That was her job!

My parents, and most parents, taught very clearly the need to take care of both parents and grandparents. For instance, my wife Donnie and her siblings would take turns taking her grandma and grandpa Batdorff to the doctors or anything else that was needed. It was just expected in those days. It is called respect. I never will forget the last trip that I took when moving to our new home on Carlisle Highway. I had left my grandparents' place on Stine Road and at the last minute, Grandma gave me a piece of old dried up bread and the driest cheese you have ever eaten (this is all she had). On the way home, I took one bite, nearly choked, but as I was taught, I still finished the sandwich because it was given by my grandparents. I would have finished that sandwich if it killed me. It is called respect.

Chapter Three
THRESHING DAY

Yes, there I was in the summer of 1938, approximately six-and-a-half years old (you had to make the halves count in those days). Waiting impatiently, I was looking through a window to the north up Chester Road to a small rise about one-quarter mile away. After all, that was where that very large threshing machine was supposed to show up. It was already 7:30 a.m., where was he?

The threshing machine, owned by Clare Ash Sr., appeared in a few minutes. It was pulled by a large Huber tractor, with a wide wheeled front end and large steel wheels at the back. The large back wheels were also steel with pegs that would grip the gravel road. The road was not paved at that time. The machine was traveling at a whopping three-miles an hour. Clare Ash Jr., who is still alive at this writing and is now 94 years old, explained the reason for this slow speed. It was because the large steel wheels with pegs would make the machine shake causing damage if it went any faster. As a matter of record, before we moved from the Vomberg farm, probably in 1942 (according to Clare Ash Jr.), the heavy peg steel wheels were changed to rubber.

In about ten minutes, the machine turned into our drive, went straight back into our barnyard, turned around and backed the machine close enough to the barn so we could fill one section of the barn with straw. The conveyor was now towards the front of the machine ready for the grain to be tossed into the feeder. By this time, the heavy drive belt had been installed on the thresher and on the flywheel of the tractor and ready to go. Sure enough, here came the first load of grain from the field. In this case, it was wheat because the wheat would be dry and ready for threshing three or four weeks ahead of the oat harvest. As a side note, if the thresher was used on larger farms, they usually came twice, once for wheat and once for oats.

Before we tossed the grain in, let's make clear that the machine was built with a blower for the straw, which was blown into the farmer's barn, or an outside straw stack. In winter months, it was much easier to get the straw down from inside the barn where it was dry, than to fight the winter winds and snow if it were outside. In our case, we did both which was quite common.

The grain bagger, where the finished product came out, had a lever, which allowed the farmer to take the one full bag of grain off while the other side was being filled up. In most cases, wheat was used for a "cash" crop, and many times was loaded onto a wagon to be taken back the following day to the country mill for sale. Frankly, it took a pretty good man to handle a two-bushel sack of wheat. Wheat weighs nearly 60 pounds per bushel, which means you were lifting about 120 pounds, which requires a bit of muscle. Oats, on the other hand, only weighs 32 pounds per bushel so a full bag was roughly 65 pounds.

By this time, the first load of grain bundles was starting to unload into the conveyor. The heads of the bundles (the grain end), always went into the machine first. There were usually between four and six wagons loading up in the field, taking their turn to get unloaded.

Interestingly enough, even little guys like me had things to do during harvest. It was often bringing cold water or lemonade to the farmers, or anyone else working on the machine, or bringing empty sacks to be filled with grain. Another job would be to tie the sacks up that would be going for "cash."

Every farmer looked forward to lunch because all farm wives tried to keep up with the "Jones" and put on a bigger spread than the neighbor across the street. Whether it was their special recipe of country fried chicken with all the trimmings, beef pot roast was also a favorite, roast turkey, or whatever else was their specialty. Of course, there was also the contest of who could bake the best cherry pie, mincemeat pie, special cake, or ice cream.

In those days, the farmers all liked to sit around a large table together. I was reminded the other day by Clare Ash Jr., that when the thresher was either at our farm or on Grandpa's, one of the hungry farmers grabbed some mashed potatoes and gravy and began to chow down. My grandpa John carefully made it clear that we hadn't said grace yet. The farmer immediately bowed his head, and removed his hat in respect as did all the other farmers. Grandpa thanked God for the blessings of the food, the hands that prepared it, and it couldn't help but be noted that every man joined in with a hardy "Amen!" Again, I just want to point out the respect shown, even by those who were not necessarily church-going people. Oh, how we miss that respect today.

Chapter Four

THE VOMBERG FARM
- SOIL PREPARATION

Before we get started, allow me to step back a couple of steps. My grandfather, John W. Clements was born in 1879, so he was already 21 at the turn of the century. He was given a brand-new pocket watch for his 21st birthday that is still in the hands of our oldest grandson, Kristopher Clements. My dad, Paul S. Clements, born in 1905, grew up on the family farm with two brothers, and it is almost hard to believe that in those days a family of five could make a reasonable living on 40 acres.

Again, for our grandchildren and great-grandchildren and all in that bracket, I'm not quite sure how I can get it across strong enough for each of them to realize the vast differences and changes that took place in the first half of the 20th century. Somewhere around the end of World War I (1918), most farms did not have indoor plumbing or electricity. This emphasizes the importance of a lantern for early morning chores and evening chores, especially in the winter months. The lantern was an absolute must. Even then the radios (if they had them), were battery-powered because of no electricity. I always turned on the radio at 6 a.m. to listen to the blind brothers, Mack and Bob, sing sincerely a song I've never forgotten called, "Did You Think to Pray?" written by Mary A. Pepper Kidder. It went:

> "Ere you left your room this morning,
> Did you think to pray?

In the name of Christ, our Savior,
Did you ask for loving favor as your shield today?

Oh, how praying rests the weary!
Prayer will change the night to day.
So, when life seems dark and dreary,
Don't forget to pray."

Now let's prepare the soil for planting. The majority of farmers had nothing but a walking plow with handles that came up, one for each hand, and even the lines that went to the horses were tied together and put around the farmer's shoulders so that both hands of the farmer were free to hang on to the plow. The horses went more by voice command than anything else. If they were to go right, the farmer would just yell, "Gee!" and to go left was, "Haw!" The plow and moldboard were usually only a single 12-inch bottom plow, and it would take a good day to plow between one-and-a-half and two acres.

Riding plows that were a single bottom 14-inch plow, could maybe gain a half-acre a day. For the record, the plows were designed to operate, at best, at a depth of approximately one-half the depth of the plow. For instance, if it were a 12-inch bottom plow, it would plow about six inches deep, if it were 14 inches it could plow approximately seven inches, and so on.

After plowing the furrow, we had to make sure that the ground was even and fit for planting. Three or four different implements were used to accomplish this. Number one was a roller that looked like two large drums, only a little larger, to crush the clods, or a cultipacker. Both instruments were between seven and eight feet wide, both also had a rack on top so you could add on a few stones or cement blocks to help crush the heavier clods. There were two other implements that were often used. The first was a drag (or harrow, depending on which state you are from) which had a lever per section and each section was roughly three feet wide. The levers were used to adjust the depth that you wanted to drag to smooth the area out. In all the ones described so far, they were usually pulled by horses. In reference to the drag, it was one horse per section, so two horses would normally pull a six-foot section. If you had a heavier team like our Dick and Joan (pronounced JoAnn), you could hook three sections together, but just not set them so deep. The last implement was a disc, which was a series of round shapes spaced about five or six inches apart and again about eight feet wide. Again, there was a lever to tilt the disc diagonally to smash the heavier clods to smaller pieces.

Usually, this process of going over the ground two or three times with a combination of a drag, disc, roller, or cultipacker would have it ready for planting. This, of course, was done first in the spring for oats and second usually for corn. In some Michigan farms, the third crop of navy beans would be planted; this was more common in the Saginaw Valley of Michigan as well as many other states.

For oats, a drill was brought in, again pulled by two horses, usually about eight feet wide and it was adjusted so that they would use about two or two-and-a-half bushels of oats per acre (or wheat if it was fall). The drill dropped down the seed into the soil with levers that would open or close to allow the grain to fall through the chute into the ground; the drill was designed to cover the seed with about two to three inches of soil. The germination time was about one week depending on how warm the weather was, and the proper amount of rain.

Concerning corn, in the early 1900s on smaller farms, they just used a hand corn planter that was jabbed into the soil after the seed was dropped into the planter. When the planter was set in the ground, the farmer would rock the planter forward and it released the seed into the ground. When the farmer removed the planter, the ground would fall over the seed. By the late twenties or early thirties, most were using a riding corn planter that would plant two rows at a time, usually 38 inches apart.

We officially started farming for the Vomberg's in January of 1938. For the record, there are two different ways for the renter to pay the owner of the farm. The first way was for both the farm owner and farm renter to put up half of the money for the seed, fertilizer, etc., then at harvest time the farm owner would get one half and the farm renter would get the other half. The second way was for the renter to put all the money upfront for the seed, fertilizer, and any other thing that was needed for preparation. Then at harvest time, the renter would get two-thirds and the farm owner one-third. The two-thirds/one-third method was the one most commonly used.

As indicated the Vomberg farm was 120 acres with a large two-story house. This farm was equipped with a very large barn, extra buildings like a storage shed, pigpen, chicken coop, sheep barn, and a grainery, and other small buildings like a well house, and, of course, the little white house at the back of the big white house. Can you imagine a time when you had to go to the bathroom in the winter months, and you had to go through heavy snow and sometimes brush the snow off the seat before you did your morning "business"?

For the record, when Dad and Mom moved in he brought some cows with him from Grandpa's that were his (about five) and then added eight to ten more. Most of our cows at that time were either Guernsey or Jersey. These were used because they had a higher butterfat content to the milk, which means there was more cream in the milk than Holstein cows which produced more milk, but had less cream content to the milk.

We started with the two main horses, Dick and Joan, as indicated, but shortly added three more middleweight horses: King, Queen, and Mollie. At that time, we had around thirty ewes and, of course, a good "crop" of lambs each spring. In the chicken coop, we had about 150 white rock hens and a couple of roosters. At that time, we had three or four sows which had two litters a year of roughly eight to ten piglets each.

Before we leave this chapter, we want to cover haying time. In other words, make hay while the sun shines. The equipment in that time, in the 1930s and 1940s, was a mower that cut a swath anywhere from six to eight feet wide with a little kicker at the end so that when you made the next round you wouldn't get clogged up with pre-cut hay. After a day or two of drying, there were two ways to windrow the hay. One was a dump rake that you would go crossways of the field and drag the hay into a predetermined linear row of hay. This was hard to keep a consistent straight line. The more common way, however, was to use a side delivery rake that would kick the hay sideways about eight to ten feet and deposit it into a straight line to be picked up by the hay loader a day or two later.

Hopefully, there would be no rain in the next three or four days if you wanted good quality hay. For the record, there were three major types of hay used on a farm. Number one, alfalfa with sometimes a little brome thrown in for volume and this was used mainly for feed to the cattle. The second one was clover and again with a little brome thrown in and again could be used for cattle, sheep, or whatever. The third type, which was mainly for the horses, was timothy and sometimes a little extra rye or other light grass was grown with it for volume. The horses did much better on this type of hay. The alfalfa especially was not digested well by the horses and could cause a problem.

When the hay was dry, we would pull in a hay loader which was hooked on the back end of the wagon and the arms (several of them), would lift the hay up the loader and deposit it on the wagon. The farmer would carefully place it so it would be easy to unload when it was taken to the barn. The children, like myself or my sister, would drive the horses from the front of the wagon over the windrows and hopefully not get buried with hay when the load was nearly full.

At the barn, would be two hay forks to lift the hay into the loft. These large tines were at least two feet wide and at least three to three-and-a-half feet long and they would be thrust into about half of the wagon (front or back), and then an internal lever would be pulled causing approximately half the wagon to be lifted up via ropes into the mow at one time. The team of horses would be hooked to a heavy one-inch rope, through a pulley that would lift the hay to the top of the barn, then shifted sideways to the approximate area where the farmer wanted it dumped. The farmer would then level it for the winter (or smooth it out). The last lift of hay would be by a sling that had been placed on the floor of the wagon before the loading began and then lifted up. And again, tripped by the farmer when it was in its proper location.

As I indicated early, my Grandpa John was a very horse-loving individual who never wanted a team to be abused. One day, when I was not more than 11 years old, I hooked Dick and Joan (the heavy team) to a cultipacker and went over a 13-acre field in slightly more than three hours by walking up the hill and making them jog on every downhill. When I brought the team to the barn the leather was over the harness by close to an inch. When Grandpa saw this and me, I got a lecturing that I never had been able to forget, and rightfully so. To make the matters worse, the following day, I had to drag the field just past where I worked yesterday, and sure enough I had the heavy team on a three-section 9-foot drag. At least I did what Grandpa wanted and was resting the team for 5 minutes on every round I was dragging. When you are dragging, you are walking all the way -- no cheating with a ride here. I mistakenly laid the lines down to take a brief rest in the shade with the horses. When I started up again, by mistake, I picked the lines up crossways; in other words, when I thought I was telling them to gee (to the right), I was forcing them to do exactly the opposite. The horses kept hawing so far to the left that they turned the drag upside down and bent all the levers. You think I was in trouble the day before? The lecture I heard from my grandpa was mild compared to what I heard from my dad this time. At 11 years old there was no way I could turn the drag right side up. It took all three of us to unhook the horses, turn the drag right side up and start over. And Dad had a terrible time straightening out the levers that I had severely bent with my carelessness. Those two days I wish I could forget. On the other hand, with the lessons learned, I would never repeat it again.

In this chapter, not only have I pointed out how to prepare the soil, but it is also necessary to say that I learned a lot of life lessons in the mistakes I've made. Just as we need to have the soil prepared to accept the seed, we also need our hearts prepared to accept the Word of God and have His seed in us to prepare us for His soon return. The Bible indicates many times the importance of preparing for the future and having our lives in order because Jesus could come at any time. The spiritual tools for this preparation include prayer, Bible study, fasting, surrendering of our will to His, and service. And just like the Psalms, we need to have an attitude of gratitude as we lift our voices in constant praise and thanksgiving.

P.S. He married the apple of his eye, just to find out it was a crab apple.

Chapter Five

THE MILKING PROCESS
IN EARLY DAYS

Back in the early days, milking by hand was the normal process, but it got the job done. The old statement goes *that the cream always rises to the top*, which simply means, if you are going to be the cream of the crop you gotta be at your best. The pail of milk was brought to a cream separator. In the early days, with no electricity, you had to crank the machine by hand, and something like skim milk would come out of the large spout, and the cream separated out through a smaller spout. After electricity, this process was done by just turning the machine on.

The cream was separated for three reasons: One, for churning for butter; two, cream for the coffee; or three, to be sold to the local creamery for cash (such as the Blue-Ribbon Creamery in Charlotte on Shephard's Street). My grandmother, Glycine, could always be found pumping the churn, bringing it from cream to butter. As a side note, most of the now skim milk was either given to the young calves being raised or given to the hogs as part of their nourishment.

Obviously, when you were milking by hand it was much more of a chore than when the milking machines were added to the barn because that involved electricity. If you didn't sell the extra cream and you wanted to sell the milk before you separated it, you could sell it as grade B milk to a company like Pet Milk. At that time, there was one located on East Henry Street, near the stockyard. Just to include it with this point, once we moved to the Chapel farm, we added more Holstein type cows and sold most of the milk as grade A, which required a very large vat of cold water. All the milk was kept in 10-gallon milk cans, immediately placed in the ice-cold water to ensure higher quality (this helped keep the bacteria levels down).

As a side note, most of the many poems I learned, I memorized while milking cows. When I would bring a pail of milk from the barn to the strainer (we then had milking machines), I would grab a line or two of poetry and by the end of the night, I would have another poem memorized. These, in turn, were used by our family and by me personally for our presentations with our music and in sermonettes.

Later, lines were installed to go directly to the coolers, stopping the tiring task of carrying the milk by hand. In later years, the standard stanchions were replaced with large milking parlors, where the cows temporarily ate their lunch while being milked. The cows were in large open areas around or near the barn and this made for a much faster process, as the milk went directly into the now large stainless-steel containers. This allowed many farmers to now keep in excess of 100 cows in their location. The hard work that I did growing up is now a very simple process, by comparison. The huge tanker trucks would pick up a large quantity every day or every other day, take it to the milk factories to be processed, sold mainly by door-to-door delivery men, or to now large supermarkets. My, how times have changed! Just as a side note, before I close this chapter, Dad and I probably milked in excess of about two million pounds of milk.

Chapter Six

VALLEY SCHOOL
- GRADES 1-6

After my kindergarten year at Millerburg school, we moved to the Vomberg Farm, which Dad rented. Our new school, for Wilma and I, was located on Chester Road, just south of Valley Highway, roughly what would be the equivalent of one block away. The school was located on the west side of the road.

The area around the schoolhouse was quite small. So, one of the farmers, across the road from the school, had graciously given us a large enough area to play softball or whatever games we had wished to do. For the record, most years the school had between 12 and 15 students. Two of the teachers I remember were Mrs. Leach and Mrs. O'Brian.

Like all kids, I looked forward to recess time. I well remember two things that happened that started on the playground. One was a softball game, where two brothers were playing against each other. The one who was in the sixth-grade was playing short-stop, and his older, stronger, taller brother was up to bat. The larger eighth-grader hit a hard, line drive softball that missed his brother's glove and hit him so hard in the stomach, he did a total backflip, jumped up, and pulled the ball from his stomach, and said, "Brother, you're out!" Strength doesn't always win.

On another occasion, the teacher Mrs. Leach was having fun with us by taking small stones, tying a knot around the stone, rolling it up, and seeing how high you could throw it in the air. We would then measure the time that it took for the little parachute to land. Obviously, if it was a small stone, it came down slowly. If it was a heavier stone, it didn't take long to land. There was however a problem. One boy, who was in the second or third grade, decided to try his own experiment at home. He climbed up on a windmill and jumped off 15 or 20 feet from the ground. He used a gunny sack to try to break his fall like our smaller parachutes. Thank God, all he ended up with was a broken arm, but that experiment stopped the teacher from ever trying that game again.

Two of our eighth-grade girls, June, and Virginia, were always up to mischief. When Halloween came, we met at one of their houses, which was on Valley Highway, about a half-mile east of Chester Road. Going roughly another quarter-mile east, there was an abandoned house with a small creek running across the road. The house hadn't been used for roughly 30 years. The girls were telling us horror stories and Halloween stories all the way up to the house. As we neared the house, there appeared a small light flickering from the old house's door. We started up the incline, and just before we got there, June said, "Look up in the tree, there is a goblin!" Which was the exact time that somebody in a white sheet jumped out the front door at us. The scramble had everyone going topsy-turvy as we tripped over each other going down the hill. As a side note, we proved it later that it was probably her dad who scared us because when we arrived back home, he was calmly reading the newspaper, pretending nothing had happened. Oh well, that is the way things happened back in those days.

One other thing before we leave Valley School. My friend Max and I were walking home one spring day and for some stupid reason, we decided to throw a stone at a big car that had just passed us going north on Chester Road. The car immediately stopped, a man got out who looked to be least six-foot-two and 250 pounds (at least he looked that big to us!) and came charging back at us. He grabbed both Max and me by the nape of our neck, shook us like a dog would a coon, and told us very strongly that he was going to tell our teacher, our parents, the local police, and all neighbors as to what we had done. Then he got back in his car and left. Needless to say, it was one of the best things that ever happened to Max and me. We never tried that stunt again.

Pun time! The Sabbath School teacher was telling her children about the story of Lot's wife. Her husband Lot, their daughters, and she were clearly told, "Don't look back!" But, Lot's wife did look back and immediately turned into a pillar of salt. A young lad raised his hand and said, "Teacher, I can understand that. While driving, my mother looked back and she turned into a telephone pole."

Chapter Seven

PEARL HARBOR -
HAWAIIAN GUITAR - PTA

December 7, 1941, is a day that will always stand in infamy. Japan bombed Pearl Harbor, Hawaii, early in the morning. There were thousands of lives lost and heavy damage and destruction to our ships. Immediately, the United States, and the world for that matter, was in World War II.

In early 1942 (probably late January or early February), I was sick on Sunday morning, and my parents thought it best that I stay at home rather than expose everyone to whatever I had. Both my sister Wilma and I had been taking Hawaiian guitar lessons from the Shamp family in Charlotte. Frankly, I spent more time practicing than my sister, mostly on old hymns and other good songs. The Hawaiian guitar, in that day, was laid flat on your lap and had a round fret bar to achieve the chords and/or melody you wanted to produce. At that time, I learned how to produce the "clink", which is a special way to strike the fret at an oblique angle and it gives a one-octave jump, producing a very special sound.

That morning, I kept myself busy playing the guitar. Even though I was not quite ten years old yet, with World War II now in full swing, I wrote my first song. It was a mother's prayer for her son who had just joined the army. The verse and chorus went like this:

"There once was a mother's boy
Who loved his home and country
But then, he was called by "Uncle Sam"
To fight the war for the cause of freedom
When his mother prayed this is what she said,

'Dear God watch over my boy in service
Dear Lord through the wilderness may he see
And when his life on earth is ended
There in Heaven may he be.'"

The song was never published but was first used at the local PTA, probably in the month of February, 1942. The PTA (Parent Teachers Association) met every month at the Valley school and the teachers would always give an update on how the children were doing and what was going on in the classroom. In those days, all those types of meetings were both opened and closed by prayer.

Because of the war, I was asked to sing this song along with some of the other parts of a small program that the teacher had arranged to present. I can remember like it was yesterday, two girls (probably second or third-grade) sang with American flags as they marched back and forth in front of the school. They were proudly singing loudly, "We did it before, and we can do it again!" Of course, this song had reference to World War I.

It is interesting to know that back then, the monthly PTAs were very well attended social gatherings, sometimes just for the update, and sometimes with light refreshment. But in all cases, there was a strong emphasis on parents, students, God, and country. The respect that was shown to our teachers and demanded by our parents is no longer an automatic duty today. Back then, *all parents*, mine included, made it very clear that if we ever got in trouble in school, the punishment would be doubled or tripled when we got home. My, how times have changed. We have lost a lot of respect for teachers, parents, grandparents, or *anyone* in authority.

Chapter Eight

A DOG NAMED ROVER

R over came into my life about the time we moved to the Vomberg
farm on Chester Road, five and a half miles northwest of
Charlotte. As dogs go, Rover was my very best friend. Rover was a
collie marked like Lassie in the story of "Lassie Come Home." He
had a beautiful white blaze down the center of his face with white
feet and lower legs white and a golden light brown coat. But Rover,
of course, was a male dog, and because of this, he was larger than
Lassie. Rover seemed to have all the instincts of a very smart dog.
Rover was extremely easy to train, always obedient, and extremely
loyal.

For instance, I took Rover a half-mile back the lane to the woodlot
where most of the cows stayed because of the shade from the trees
and the lush grass and water holes. I would point out the lagging
cows with a mild command to bring the cow or cows forward
towards the barn. All I needed to do was give a mild command and
Rover would give a light bark and nip the cows in the heels to let
them know he was boss, but never hurt them. Rover, occasionally
would get a little rough and I would mildly scold him but also praise
him when I felt he was doing the corralling correctly.

Within one or two weeks, Rover got the message and all I had to
say was, "Rover, it's time to bring the cows up from the pasture for
milking" and just point back the lane. He would leave the barnyard,
head back the lane, and within fifteen or twenty minutes the cows
would all come marching forward like soldiers in a parade. I would
open the door to the cow barn and just stand back and Rover would

start directing the cows into their own stalls. How he knew this, I don't have a clue. All I had to do was just go in and lock them into a stanchion.

Rover soon taught all the animals to obey him, but the only animals he had trouble with were the sheep. Sheep are usually led by a shepherd, going all the way back to Bible days and David. Rover never hurt them but appeared to be flustered that everything else he could drive but the sheep did not want to cooperate.

To prove the point, in the slower months of the winter (about fifteen years later), I would work at the local livestock auction helping to drive all the calves, cows, pigs, sheep, bulls, and horses through the ring to be sold. No problem with any of them, except the sheep. Oddly enough, if I grabbed a ewe by the leg and gently pulled her forward, all the sheep would then follow. (JOKE - Question: Why did the ram go over the cliff. Answer: He never saw the ewe turn).

Basically, Rover proved to be an outdoor dog, usually staying in the tool shed or barn at night to protect our buildings. The only exception was in the winter months when we would bring Rover into the back room of the house so it wouldn't be quite so cold for him.

As a side note, late one fall day, my uncles Lester and Howard (my mother's brothers) had been coon hunting and, for whatever dumb reason, had shot a skunk. They came to the tool shed to get a bag to put the skunk in to lessen the smell. They started to go in the shed; Rover met them at the door, growled, showed his teeth, and for some reason, they decided not to get the bag. Rover protected everything that was ours, and made sure no one was going to trespass, unless we gave him the okay.

On most large farms, the butchering of heavy beef and other animals was done by the farmer. A beef carcass was very heavy, so they would hook the two hind legs to the heavy ropes (also used when they were unloading hay), lift it so it would clear the floor by at least a foot above the front legs, leave the barn doors open so the carcass would air out, and we would just tell Rover that he was on guard for the night. We would go to sleep at night even though the expensive beef was clearly seen from the road, knowing we had nothing to worry about.

Interestingly enough, however, if Dad cut off a little bit of the front leg (mostly bone) gave it to Rover and told him it was his, no one -- including us, ever thought to take it away. It was his! I can't say Rover was exceptionally smart because dogs don't have the reasoning power that we have. So, let's just say he had the most natural instincts ever given a dog.

The lady of the home was always busy cold-packing the meat from the butchering as well as canning vegetables, like tomatoes and so forth. Although most farms did not have refrigerators (because of no electricity), they usually had an icebox. The icebox would keep food for a short period of time in place of a refrigerator. Most cities like Charlotte would have frozen food lockers that you could rent. In Charlotte, it was the Palmer Storage, and in Sunfield it was Hannah, and there would be like ones in all small towns. All the beef, pork, lamb, and other meats that were butchered would be processed by the locker owner, packaged according to your discretion, and would be placed in your locker. There would be two keys, one for the locker owner, and one for you, so that you could get to your meats when you needed to. The farmer would bring home enough for a week or so every time he went to the mill. Most storage lockers were in the mill areas of the city. Again, the icebox would keep the meat well enough while it was thawing, which really did two things: one, the frozen chunks of meat kept the icebox cool and two, the icebox would keep the meat good for a week to ten days.

One of the saddest days of my life was when we were moving from the Vomberg farm in late 1942 or early 1943. A terrible thing happened. I was driving the heaviest team of horses, Dick and Joan, on a corn binder, taking it to the new location on Carlisle Highway. Just over one-half of a mile from the new home, a car at high speeds swung around me, intentionally went into the grass, and killed Rover within 30 feet of my eyesight. I have never been able to forget that day. – Tell me, why would anyone spend their youth seeing how many dogs they could kill with cars, like notches on a western gun? I just don't understand why. I'll never understand. – What a dog. What a companion. What a friend was Rover!

Chapter Nine

FARMING FROM THEN TO NOW

I'm sorry, there is one thing I meant to mention on early wages that I forgot to tell you, so let's put it in now. A church member of ours, Will Lafrey, would walk from Charlotte to our farm which was about five and a half miles, grab a corn sickle cutter and start to cut down eight rows of corn at a time and start to put them around a long sawhorse. The corn's height would be between eight and nine feet. The sawhorse would have two legs in front which would come up from either side and would stand about four feet tall at the front, then a long two-by-four about 12 feet long would be hooked to the front and angled down and back to the ground. Again, back to the front, for the tall part of the sawhorse, they would use a broomstick, and it probably was to lean the tall corn against from all four sides. When the shock or bundle was large enough, Will would climb up, and tie a binder tie tightly around it. He would pull the broomstick out, which would now allow the sawhorse to be pulled to the next location. As a side note, when you cut the corn in the fall, it is not usually quite ripe enough or dry enough so it would need some more curing. The farmer would then either husk the corn late in the fall in the field, or bring it to the barn and work on it inside during winter days where it was not quite so cold. Now to the part you will not quite understand, Will would work at least eight hours, walk back into town and his pay for the day was one dollar. Not an hour, but *total*. And frankly, he was glad to get it. My how times have changed!

Most of our earlier chapters on farming covered from the turn of the century till about the end of World War II, so we want to put in a chapter to "bring you up to date" so to speak of the changes of what has happened from 1945 until today. I indicated earlier that because of all the time, effort, and money spent on the war, on tanks, jeeps, ammunition, and so forth, there were very few tractors available until after the war. So when we left off with our earlier coverage on farming, most of the farm work had been done by horses, threshing machines, small one or two-plow tractors at best, but *now* the majority of tractors were getting into the next stage where they could pull three, four, or five bottom plows. At the same time, the threshing machine and crews became nearly obsolete in a reasonably short period of time because the combines were soon taking their place. First pulled by a tractor, but then motorized, so they became self-sufficient. Although they started with a six-foot width of cutting, today many of them are from 40 to 45 feet wide.

The same thing was happening not only with the tractor but also with other machinery. Suddenly, these small disks, drag, roller, or cultipacker were now either made much larger, or the farmers would hook two or three of them together to prepare the soil once instead of going over the soil three or four times before planting. Again, by the 1960s or 1970s, disk plows were gradually replacing the standard plows. In other areas, drills, corn planters, and other machines were also increasing in size. For instance, the corn rows which used to be from 36-38 inches, are now down to 30 inches. I noticed last year that a neighbor had a 24-row corn planter. Ten on the left-ring, ten on the right, and four in back. In other words, he was planting a width of 60 feet wide at a time. I could not believe my eyes that you could plant 24 rows at once! Wow! The corn combine in the fall would do eight-rows at a time that both husked and shelled the corn and would take the load of this cash crop to the elevator. One machine could do it all!

Of the nearly one hundred years, between my dad and my life span, farming has drastically changed. When I realize that my grandmother and grandfather successfully raised a family of five on 40 acres, now blows my mind. If Grandpa was alive today, I'd have to give him oxygen to bring him back to reality.

Chapter Ten

HOW SWEET IT IS

In eastern states like Michigan, Vermont, and several other states the early days of late winter or early spring were dominated by making maple syrup. The "hard" maple or sugar maple, that has been frozen during the wintertime, gives up a sweet sap during the thawing. When early spring or late winter days change, with night temperatures in the 20s to mid-30s, the roots of the hard maple start sending sap upward. This is to nourish the branches for the new spring and summer of growth with abundant leaves.

Usually, in late February or early March, this process begins. The early "run" of sap usually gives off the best quality with a light amber color, an excellent taste, and is preferred by most people as being nearly perfect. While tapping the trees, there are two things to remember: one, the tree size to determine whether it should be tapped for one, two, or three buckets; and two, look for larger heavier roots going down because obviously the heavier flow of sap comes up through those roots. It is best for the smaller trees not to be tapped because they are dependent on all the sap for additional tree growth. Although some maple syrup farmers would disagree, it is usually not advisable to tap trees under 16 to 18 inches in diameter. Usually, one bucket per tree is used from the approximate 18 inches to 26 or 28 inches. Two buckets are used on larger trees from 28 to 38 inches in diameter. A few of the trees, in excess of 40 inches, are large enough to use three buckets, at the tapper's discretion. It is possible to over tap, which could be detrimental to the health of the tree.

In the early days, trees were tapped with a hand drill. The

bit size usually used was 15/32, just under half an inch, the drill hole would be about 3/4 inches deep, with a slight upward slant of approximately ten degrees to assist in the natural flow of sap into the bucket. The spigot needs to be tapped in with a hammer (preferably rubber) to be snug but not overdriven.

The sap usually starts to flow around 34 degrees Fahrenheit. It flows quite freely between 35-40 degrees. Because of the change of season, there may still be snow on the ground. On the underside of the spigot, there is a hook for the bucket to catch the sap. These buckets run from 12 to 16 quarts in size (usually). Depending upon the amount of sunshine and how fast the temperature rises, the bucket will typically be filled up with a constant *drip, drip, drip* in less than a day.

Earlier, I mentioned that the large syrup bush farmers start early depending on if they have 100 bucket bush or larger. If by any chance, there is an extremely cold period of a week or two, the tap hole may tend to start to dry up. In that case, you need to remove the spigot and use a reamer to refresh the hole. Obviously, don't over ream or the spigot won't stay in.

The sweetness of the sap can vary from year to year. Normally it takes around 35 gallons of sap when boiled down it gives you approximately one gallon of syrup. In excellent years, I've seen the sap to syrup ratio as low as a 26-to-one.

In the early years, before 1930, a very large pan was used, roughly four feet square and approximately 12 inches deep. The problem with this type of boiling was that the timing was critical to remove the very hot pan because if left too long the syrup could become crystallized. This is a two-man operation, and the timing is extremely critical.

Shortly thereafter, though some evaporators were used prior to that time, the use of very large evaporators became quite common. These were sophisticated enough that the raw sap went in one end, and after going through a series of channels, processed-syrup came out the other end. An average size, four feet wide and 15 feet long, will boil out at least 30 to 40 gallons of raw sap per hour. In most cases, the early evaporator did not have a constant flow of finished syrup. A couple of times an hour, the farmer would drain through the spigot a smaller quantity (a few quarts). This process was called *syrupping-off*. This can vary depending on two things: the size of the evaporator and the amount of wood or fuel being used. A syrup thermometer was usually kept right nearby and checked every few minutes. At that point, a spigot is opened to syrup-off the syrup, usually into a ten-gallon milk can (or something similar). The syrup was strained through a heavy felt filter which was necessary to take the sugar sand out of the syrup. Be mindful that these early runs of sap give a better-quality maple syrup as *long as the sap is immediately boiled down and not allowed to sit around for a few days.* It is critical to mention that the temperature needs to be very closely controlled between 215-217 degrees Fahrenheit. Note, if it is under 215 degrees, many times the syrup is not quite heavy enough to last a long time without mold, and on the other end if you go too high it starts to turn to sugar.

Over the years, the business of gathering sap has changed tremendously. In the early 1900s, many times it would be nothing more than a sleigh or wagon that contained 55-gallon drums. The farmer gathered the sap from each individual tree, carried it to the wagon, and pour the sap through funnels into the heavy drums. The problem with this process, however, is twofold. You must unload these heavy drums (400 or more pounds) from the wagon and then get the drums elevated above the large holding tanks so that it would allow a natural gravity flow into the evaporator. Try taking 400 pounds barrels, rolling them carefully up high enough on the ice-covered rails, and getting them unloaded without "losing" them. This is a critical art!

The large holding tanks have a faucet that would normally be set for constant flow that would be the equivalent of how fast the sap was boiled off. Most evaporators were fueled by precut wood (cut the previous summer) and sometimes made hotter by a few lumps of coal or kerosene. Our operation compared to others was quite small, as we tapped about 350 buckets. So, for us, it was collecting sap all day by horses, buggies, or other means, and then we would run the evaporator starting from noon until well into the night so that the sap did not get "old."

Later on, when our children were young, we also helped my

wife's father at their farm in Sunfield. After working all day at the shop, we'd head to Sunfield, and quickly gather more sap until pitch dark. We would usually take some hot dogs, sweet corn, or something else and throw it into the raw end of the sap. May I say, right here is where you *really* get "sweet corn!" As the night wore on, we would put the kids to bed under the edge of the evaporator to take a nap until we were ready to go home. The extra warmth thrown off by the evaporator would put them to sleep almost immediately. We would have to blanket them up, head to the car, and take them home and put them to bed, while dad had three-quick-winks before he headed back to his regular job. We would do this six days a week, not get home until 1:30 or so in the morning, sleep three or four hours and start the rotation all over again. Tons of work, yet still lots of fun!

Things have really changed in the last 30 or 40 years. In most cases now, on the larger operations, there are collecting lines going directly from the hillside trees to a collecting station at the bottom where the sap is then taken directly to the evaporator. I guess I would have to admit, I wouldn't know how to handle this new process, with all the sweat of hauling the buckets to the barrels. As a closing note, back in our day, we were fortunate if we got between $3 and $4 a gallon for the syrup. Today, that same gallon of syrup would run from $35 to $50 depending on the location, quality, or demand.

There is one area of fun that we use to have that seems to be missing today. In our day, the Sunday school or Sabbath school classes of young people would get together and have sugar offs. This simply means you would take the maple syrup, put it on the stove, intentionally bring it past the syrup stage, put it in a bowl, and stir it until it became sugar candy, either soft or hard. Laughingly, the maple sugar was so sweet my wife's mother would offer the recipients dill pickles to cut the taste! I must tell you, those days were special, and something that seems to be missing today.

Pun: Remember - Keep your words sweet - You might have to "eat" them.

Chapter Eleven
4H AND THE COUNTY FAIR

Growing up, I spent quite a few years in the 4H Club (Head, Heart, Hands, and Health). In doing so, we would have monthly meetings, starting at different farmer's homes. In some ways, it was similar to a PT meeting, but just no teachers. One of our members was Roger Smith, whose parents were Mr. and Mrs. Cloman Smith, and they had a farm two miles west of us on Carlisle Highway. This was in the war years and after. This particular meeting probably would have been 1945 or 1946. At that time, TVs were barely thought of, and if two percent of the farms had a TV it would probably be stretching the truth.

I can remember the evening like it was yesterday, because especially all the dads wanted to listen to the Joe Lewis Heavy Weight Boxing Match, and he was the champion. His opponent was Jersey Joe Walcott. Oddly enough, his real name was Arnold Cream Jr. You can see, if he wanted to become a heavyweight champ, why he didn't want to use the name "Cream."

Most of our 4H'ers had dairy, a few with sheep and swine. Those three were the main animals at the time; later there was more emphasis on horses, ponies, chickens, goats, rabbits, and birds. There were three styles of horses: riding, racing, and draft horses for pulling.

One of the individuals from another club was Stan Haigh. Interestingly enough, Stan worked for me at Carefree for several years in the 1960s and 1970s. An excellent man, competitor, and friend. In 1946, I had a Guernsey cow that took the championship. Stan beat me out for the next two years, 1947 and 1948. In order to "catch-up" with him, I had to change to a better cow and won again in 1949. So, between us, we took the Guernsey championship for four years. We also competed in the same four years for Grand Showmanship, which would indicate how well our cow was trained. Again, we split it, two years for Stan, and two years for me. We maintained a super friendship, even though when we stepped in the ring, it became highly competitive!

In modern times (the last 20 years), most of the entertainment in front of the grandstand are heavy trucks, tractors, super-eights, along with demolition derby (the smashing up of old cars). In my day, however, the entertainment was horse pulling contests with two classes of horses. The lightweight horse teams would be under 3,000 pounds, and the heavyweight edition would be in excess of 4,000 pounds and many times as high as 4,600 pounds per team.

Lloyd Bacon had a heavy resistance machine called a dynamometer. In order to reach the next weight level, the team would have to draw the machine a minimum of 21 or 22 feet. If they made the grade, they would advance to the next level for a heavier lift. This was very popular back then; many of the teams would come not only from Michigan, but also from Ohio, Illinois, and Indiana.

On another evening, they would also have a mule pulling contest and they were usually hooked to a stone boat (flat bottom), which was loaded with cement blocks that were either added on or taken off depending on the weight of the mule team. Sometimes, they even had pony pulling contents. The parades would even feature some of the contest winners.

The standard at the 4H fair was harness racing, where they would use a sulky and would run twice around the track, which would make the race one mile. My wife Donnie and I still go to harness racing today, when they are available. We laughingly bet one another to see who can pick the most race winners.

Once or twice a week they would have Shetland pony races, where they would start back by the cattle barns and would finish in front of the grandstands, not quite a quarter-mile. An interesting thing happened in one of these races. My second cousin Dexter had a very fast pony who was very hard to control. When the gun sounded for the start, the pony turned around and went about 40 yards in the wrong direction. Dexter somehow got her turned around and headed back, but by this time they were about 60 to 80 yards behind. Believe it or not, she was so fast, she still won the race even with that much of a handicap!

Another feature of the fair was also a couple of different types of parades. My younger brother Darrell (seven years younger than I), had several horses as a hobby (mostly Belgium). He hooked up four to six horses for that parade as well as the parades downtown for Memorial Day, Labor Day, and Fourth of July. Darrell knew much more about horses and their harnesses than I did, because when I was growing up, I was not tall enough to harness the big farm horses. He had this hobby as a grown man; he knew all about bridals, horse collars, hame straps, horse tugs, etc. He also would give rides during these special occasions to anyone who wanted a ride. To clarify, when I said he had like a six-horse hitch, that would be two horses three deep. You had to know how to put the lines between all your fingers, in order to control all three sets of horses. Darrell gradually changed from Belgium to the Clydesdale breed which is the same style of horses you see on the Budweiser commercials today. He sold the last Clydesdale to the people who owned the horses at Bush.

Most fairs today aren't nearly as popular as they were in the 1940-1980s. I'm not sure whether it is because there is just too much going on, or if they have simply lost their appeal. It is always great to get the large sack of caramel corn, homemade pie, or other special goodies that were available at the fair. The fair provided a sense of belonging, friendship, responsibility, and good clean competition needed by our young people.

Chapter Twelve

THE VALLEY OF THE SHADOW OF DEATH

Taken from the 23rd Psalm, but I guess for
humor sake – No way to diet

After our move to the Chapel Farm on Carlisle Road, in what would be January or February of 1943, my health began to give me serious problems. Although I was 11 years old at that time and would be 12 at the end of March, I weighed 120 pounds. No, I was not overweight or fat, but because of the heavy farm work as a boy, I was very muscular and solid. Eating was fast becoming a serious problem with heavy pains in the stomach and bowel area. I was hospitalized in the old Hayes Green Beach hospital in the last few days of April or at the latest, the first few days of May. I was 12 years old at the time. Dr. Lester Sevener, who was an excellent doctor and was very good in the diagnostic area, tried everything he could think of to get to the bottom of my problems, but soon felt it necessary to bring in a specialist for assistance and consulting. For that reason, Dr. Wilinski was brought in. He was considered to be the best specialist in this area of expertise for the state of Michigan.

The staff and doctor estimated that I had lost about half of my weight, down to about 60 pounds. Frankly, I looked like the picture of the starved African children, with at least an inch and a half cavity between each rib. I could not keep anything down and the doctors decided between them, the only way to find this extreme obstruction was to push a large tube down my throat. I said, "No way! If anyone is going to push a large 3/8-inch tube down my throat, it will be me!" After severe gagging, I pushed the tube down 17 feet. The doctors had installed a balloon on the end of the tube and now blew it up so they knew where to operate. What a scientific move!

Before the operation took place, and after extremely heavy prayer by the church, family, neighbors, friends, and so forth, Dr. Sevener was also praying, and talked to my parents. He advised my parents if, by any chance I lived 48 hours, he and Dr. Wilinski gave me a 50-50 chance of living. For the record, Dr. Sevener prayed with my parents as well as over me before the surgery.

The surgeon, Dr. Wilinski, found that my small intestine had grown inside my large intestine by nearly two feet, which had caused a complete shutdown. They removed the area of both small and large intestine, and sewed the two side by side anastomesia, for about five or six inches. Though it worked at that time, it wasn't long before the ends of the intestines, where they had been sewed, became infected. They would fill up with blood and heavy junk that over the years it would cause me to bleed rectally. The end result was that the same two surgeons, 30 years later in 1974, redid the surgery, cut out the section that had been joined laterally and hooked them up end to end as they are today.

Because of the seriousness of this situation, once the operation was over, I got over 60 meals in a row with nothing but hot tea and beef bouillon broth with no solids in any of it. At this point, I still could not handle heavy foods. During that time the nurses would come in and say laughingly that they wanted to use my washboard (my ribs) to do their washing. After about two-and-a-half or three weeks, they carried me to the scales and said that, because I was mostly now filled up with fluid, I weighed a whopping 79 pounds.

When I finally left the hospital, after my long stay, we stopped by my great-grandma Sarah Jane Stratton, known as Jenny to most people. She also lived on South Sheldon Street, not far from where my mom and dad lived early on. My great grandmother threw her arms carefully around me and stated, "I felt so useless, all I could do was pray!" Only eternity will tell, I may still be alive today because of my great grandmother who truly knew how to pray.

During that time, both my dad and mother had not only continued to pray, but frankly spent so much time at the hospital that all Dad had time for, were the daily operations such as chores, milking, feeding, and so forth. My dad had very little time to spend in the field getting the soil ready for planting. At least two, if not three or four, neighbors pitched in. Neighbor number one, Harold "Shorty" McConnell (about 5'2"), (whose son, Max, was my closest friend that lived across from us when we were on Chester Road) came with his two-bottom plow tractor. Harold Root, who owned the Blue-Ribbon Creamery on Shepherd Street in Charlotte, also joined with a two-plow tractor, and prepared two large fields, one for oats and one for corn, and got them ready for planting. I believe I am correct, that Dalton LaMonte, our new neighbor across the road on Carlisle, and I think one other man, I can't remember the name, assisted.

My dad was always willing to help assist by doing anything possible for other people. Well, it sure paid off this time! All my dad had to do was hook up the grain drill and corn planter, and in two days with their help did more than he could accomplish in ten days. With friends like that, it's great to know that we can be appreciated, and the favor returned has never been forgotten.

Now a very interesting sequel. My wife Donna was born with a total bowel obstruction and could not keep anything down for the first ten days of her life. She had also come to the point of being at death's door if something wasn't done immediately. According to her parents, their local doctor, Dr. Hyke, had asked for a specialist, whose name we don't have. Her parents were told, just as were mine, that death was imminent if the correction couldn't be found immediately. Prayer for her, with all parties concerned (church, friends, family, and others) were just as strong as mine. At ten days old, they laid her on the operating table, took out all her intestines (because they were totally twisted up), straightened them out, and tucked them back in her little body. This was at the St. Lawrence Hospital in Lansing. To my wife's young embarrassment, all her relatives kept insisting, "Let us see your scar!" Because of the operation, as such a young baby, the scar was huge and frankly not very pleasant to see. How interesting, that two totally unrelated people, would marry, and have the same powerful results of prayer. Neither of us would be here, or the story of our family, without total faith and trust in God.

Chapter Thirteen

GENERAL CONFERENCE - HARRISBURG, PENNSYLVANIA

A t 16 years of age, along with singing with the Clements Family, I started doing a lot of solo work. Therefore, after graduation in 1950, between then and when I was married to my lovely bride in 1955, I made several appearances all over Michigan, Ohio, Indiana, and other states. On many occasions, I was accompanied by a very good, young piano player, Mary Esther King who played for me whenever close enough and when available. She was so incredible that her excellent accompaniment made my job much easier and more relaxing.

In the spring of 1953, I was asked by the Michigan Conference of the United Brethren to be the featured soloist at the National Convention. Mary Esther, later became my wife's sister-in-law when she married Howard Jr. Batdorff. We were driven there by Rev. Milan Maybe, who was also a minister in our conference. Mary Esther asked her aunt Margaret along for the ride. I sang many songs, but the only two that jump to my mind at this time are, "Stranger of Galilee" and "I Will Pilot Thee," and I also gave the poem "Ol' Zion."

The main thing that sticks out in my mind, from when we were in the foothills of Pennsylvania, is that I decided it would be special to get up at sunrise and go into the foothills, find a big rock, and pray as Jesus did early in the morning. Surprise! Surprise! When I left my room, I found that it had been dripping rain all night. I decided to not let that bother me; if Jesus could pray in the rain, so could I.

I left that morning, I looked out in front of where we were staying, and there on the tennis court, rain and all, was Bishop Funk with an umbrella in one hand and Bible in the other. He was marching around the court just like it wasn't even raining. At that moment, I knew where the power that I had heard him preach was coming from. No wonder God's word says, in Isaiah 30:15, "In quietness and confidence will be your strength." Just like I was impressed earlier with his comment about emotion which said, "I'm only concerned with how straight your feet walk when they come back to earth." I had no question at that time, why he could preach the way he did. Truly a man filled with the Holy Spirit. I trust that most of the people that attended that conference left as blessed as I was.

Chapter Fourteen

CLEARING THE WOODLOT

S hortly after we moved to the Chapel Farm on Carlisle Road, my dad decided to clear away about seven acres of a woodlot. The area had been partially cleaned by the previous owner. There remained at least 40 or 50 mature trees scattered over the seven acres.

My dad asked Howard Royston, who only lived about three miles away, to help him with this large project. Uncle Howard was my mother's older brother. My mom had three brothers and three sisters, all of whom were older because she was the "baby" of the family.

In those days, most of the work was done by hand. For example, a large 66 tooth heavy cross-cut saw (that totaled about five and a half feet) was used, along with axes, chisels, and other like tools. Much of the work was done in the early winter of 1943, and was finished early in the winter of 1944. Dad tried to hurry it up to achieve spring planting in 1944. Once the trees were cut down by the hand cross-cut saw, all the limbs, four to 15 inches in diameter, were cut about 16 feet long and stacked in our lane, which was about 300 yards long. The next step was to bring in a buzz saw, with a 30-inch blade, hooked up to the pulley of a small tractor, our BN Farmall. The larger blocks of wood were split by hand with malls, axes, and/ or chisels; in other words, anything larger than the limbs that had been deposited in our lane.

My sister Wilma and I had the job to tail the buzz saw, which simply means, that after Dad had cut the limbs to about 16 inches in length, we would take the pieces of wood and throw them into huge piles, waiting for the larger ones to be split and stacked into face cords. A face cord simply means lengths of wood about 16 inches, stacked four feet high and eight feet long. It's hard to believe, but during that time we had accumulated almost 400 face cords of wood! The stacking was required so, when we sold it by the cord, they knew how much to take. Secondly, during the hot summer months the wood could dry out making it easier to burn and give hotter results to the fire. Now, in this case, some of the cords were used in our making of maple syrup, but the rest of the cords were sold as a "Cash Crop" to help both my dad, and to pay uncle Howard his share. When you consider that today, dried hard maple, beech, oak, and others (whether delivered or picked up) would sell for $45-65 per cord but back in those days, we were lucky to get $3.5 to $4 per cord. As a side note, that huge number of limbs that went over the buzz saw had been hauled into place by horses, in most cases our heavier team of Dick and Joan. I would be remiss if I didn't say that in quite cold winter days, that the heavy work that my dad, sister, and I did, would keep us warm, almost sweaty. Our hands were about the only area of the body that was hard to keep warm for two reasons, because of the roughness of the wood, our gloves would tear and fall apart quite easily, and of course, hands are more susceptible to cold anyway.

Now back to the work of the large cross-cut saw and how important it was to get a smooth rhythm of long strokes that would almost make the saw "sing." Dad and Uncle Howard had the process down pat and made it look easy. Apparently, my rhythm to take long easy strokes was nowhere near as good as Dad's or Uncle Howard's, because my dad would constantly say, "Why don't you get off and walk, stop riding the saw." I guess you could say, sooner or later, my "rhythm" improved and Dad could cut almost as fast with me as with Uncle Howard.

One of the last jobs in clearing the woodlot needed the help of an expert. Dad's friend Murray was known in the county as the "dynamiter." Murray would "plant" sticks of dynamite in the right spots under the largest roots of the stump, run a cable back about 100 feet away and ignite the sticks of dynamite. The boom was loud enough it could easily be heard from four or five miles away. The farmers around would say, "Well, I guess Murray is back to work!"

The large stumps were hooked onto a large team of horses, and the stumps were either dragged or rolled onto a stone-boat and hauled, in our case, to a low area of what was left of the woodlot. Later these stumps were covered with dirt like they used to bury stone piles. The good news about this project was that the seven acres became one of our most productive fields.

One area we need to cover is that, to the immediate west of the cleared woodlot, was a creek that opened in the middle of our farm. The creek was only about eight to ten feet wide, and in many cases, not more than a foot deep. This creek started from miles of tile that drained from the east, north, and west to the creek opening. The creek ran diagonally for about three-eighths of a mile to cross underneath Carlisle Road, right at the west end of our property.

Our creek had "tons" of muskrats and some mink. One of our local pastors, Pastor Beardsley, loved to trap the muskrats and mink during the fall and winter months. This was his second favorite job that he enjoyed doing. It would not be uncommon for him to trap 10 to 15 muskrats per week. These skinned, dried, cured pelts were worth about $3 or $4 each. Pastor Beardsley also caught one or two mink per season and, even back then, the cured mink pelt was worth $30-$35 (now you know why mink coats are so expensive). My wife's younger brother, Deb, also trapped muskrats near my wife's home in Sunfield (about 20 miles away). Their creek was not nearly as productive as ours, and Deb, at this juncture of the street, was not more than 13 to 15 years old. He and Pastor Beardsley would swap stories, and he told his dad (my father in law), that the pastor was exaggerating his stories. I guess it was hard for Deb to understand that his endeavors were not as productive as Pastor Beardsley's, and I hate to say it, but there were times that even we thought his descriptions were hyperboles.

The other area I wanted to cover was that my dad had an unusual gift of accepting things that would deeply hurt most other people. Allow me to explain. The following summer, I believe in 1945, we planted a 13-acre field of navy beans, on the east side of our farm. Dad and I not only cultivated the field three or four times, but Dad wanted it even cleaner than that, so we hoed the entire 13 acres by hand. Quite frankly, Dad was quite competitive, as well as a hard worker. He would take one row of beans, while my sister Wilma and I took a row between us and you guessed it, we were the ones having a hard time keeping up with Dad! The bean crop grew very well, except in late July or early August, when rain was needed. We went between four and five weeks without a drop of rain while the beans were flowering, but not setting, as the blossoms all dropped off. Then as the statement goes, "too little, too late," we got a nice rain. The beans set well, but because of the loss of over a month of time, the pods did not mature enough when an early frost killed them dead in the middle of September.

To my heartbroken surprise, Dad pulled the disk in the following morning and disked under that beautiful field of half mature beans and planted it to wheat the next day. I admit, after all that work, my sister and I were heartbroken. My dad, with his usual *taking things in stride* attitude, just simply said, "As long as all problems stay in the field or the barn, with God's help we can handle it." In other words, don't let these things ruin your life, take them in stride, and with Paul's admonition in the Bible *just keep on keeping on.*

The story goes that a man lost all his hair when finally, the last few hairs dropped off. Three or four months later, a friend of his caught him emptying his pockets, and guess what, a comb dropped out! The friend turned to the baldheaded man and said, "What's this?" His answer, "I just can't part with it."

Chapter Fifteen

THE SAWDUST TRAIL AND THREE CAMPGROUNDS

The United Brethren (UB) church had their campground on Sebewa Road, two or three miles north of Sunfield, Michigan. For the record, it still stands today, though it has been sold a couple of times to other churches. And yes, believe it or not, the isles of the sanctuary, at that time, were sawdust. The campmeetings were usually in August, and we had excellent speakers. When I was very little, Dr. Clyde Meadows was our Bishop and conducted many services. My favorite poet was, Lon Woodrum, the same author who wrote, "Harvest in the Tempest" and "Ol' Zion." My favorite musicians in those days were Paul and Ruth Johnson and their daughter Marilyn. Paul both wrote the song, "One of These Days" and when they sang it as the trio it would bring tears to your eyes.

Later, probably my favorite Bishop was Ezra Funk, a powerful speaker. I have never forgotten the day when some of the more energetic people would get a little carried away. He stopped his message, stood perfectly still for what seemed to be a minute or more, and then he said, "I don't care how loud you shout or how high you jump, I only care how straight your feet walk when they hit the ground." Donna's grandfather, Rev. J. I. Batdorff, was basically a very conservative man, but there were times that even he got inspired by the Holy Spirit, and his way of letting off "steam" was to pull a white hankie from his pocket, stand up, whirl the white hankie around and just say, "Whoopee!" And, it was real. You would know he had been blessed. The average attendance on a Sunday was between 1,500-2,000 people. Both my wife's family, the Batdorff Trio, and the Clements' family, sang several times at the campmeetings. I was converted when I was either 11 or 12. No, I'm not positive which, and was baptized in the Sebewa Creek that was on the east edge of the property, about 1/8 mile east of the tabernacle.

The second campmeeting was the Seventh-day Adventist (SDA) campmeeting located on highway M43 in Grand Ledge, Michigan. All our children went to the academy there in Grand Ledge for grades 9-12. On Sabbaths, it was not unusual to have crowds of 10,000-15,000. We were known as "tent city" during those ten days. I was told that there were at least 1,500 large tents on the campground. In the early-mid 1970s, the Clements Family, which was now my wife's and my family, was privileged to sing several numbers just prior to the main meeting. We immediately were followed by singers from the King's Heralds, and HMS Richards, which were both from the Voice of Prophecy Radio Ministry out of California. This radio ministry is one of the oldest radio programs in the United States. I believe they started in 1925. Many of the songs that our son's (Sim and Mike) quartet "Four for the Master" sang, were patterned after the tight barbershop harmony used by the "King's Heralds." Sadly, the campgrounds were sold and moved to the new Cedar Lake Campgrounds (which will be in the next section as campground three).

The present campground, which is the Great Lakes Adventist Academy (GLAA), is in Cedar Lake, near Edmore, Michigan, just off Highway M46. The crowds, though not so large, base their main gathering in the gym. There are several outlining large tents used for children's programs, similar to the tents used in Grand Ledge. Although there are quite a few family-sized tents, they are nothing compared to Grand Ledge, where there were then 1,500 tents. These are replaced mainly with RV units, either motorized or the popup version. As a side note, many of our grandkids received their 9-12th grade education here at GLAA. Not to interject business with church, my second job as I got towards retirement, was replacing regular windows with the new 7/8 inch insulated vinyl style windows with Low-E glass on the outer pane, with argon gas between the panes, and warm edge technology in the spacer. The warm edge technology simply means there is no aluminum or other materials that allow the frost point to jump across to the inner pane of glass. I replaced all the windows in both the boys' and girls' dormitories, as well as the church and many of the teachers' homes. The total of these projects was well over 300 windows. For the installation of these products, our son Mike worked full time as well as our friend John Lewis, Sim part-time (on weekends), and to help the students I hired about ten, letting them do such things as unwrapping, installing, hauling away, cleaning up, etc. They could either get a check or have the amount applied to their school bill.

In recent years, we have had many excellent speakers at the GLAA location for campmeeting in Cedar Lake. Many names like Doug Bachelor, John Bradshaw, Mark Finley, and Shawn Boonstra have given powerful messages. Both our family, and especially our quartet, have sung there many times, as well as others in our family.

There is no question that whether it was myself or someone else, the good old fashion campmeetings have been a blessing for all who have attended. It is one thing to have morning devotions, and the fellowship with the local church, but that ten days set apart for campmeeting is something that should be experienced by all churches and all Christian people. The blessings I have received from these can never be measured.

Chapter Sixteen
CHURCH ON FIRE (HOLY SMOKE!)

In the winter months after high school (1950 till after I was married in 1955), I worked at second jobs, either day or night shifts, anything to pick up extra money in the slower farming months. At the time mentioned here, I was working at Maynard Coupling in Olivet. On my way home Thursday, February 17, 1955, I was told that my church was completely destroyed by fire. The United Brethren in Christ Church was located across from what was the old high school on the southwest corner of Horatio Avenue and Seminary Street. Today, it doesn't look like there is enough space for a church to sit there, but it came right up to the edge of the sidewalk and within 20 feet of the parsonage; this is the first house which would be south on the same side of the street. The parsonage was saved from the fire, and still stands today.

What a shock to me! The church that I grew up in, which was a brick structure, was all gone, except for some of the bricks. All those memories of church and Sunday school, revival meetings, songfests, testimonies, and prayer meetings, were now nothing but memories. Rev. Earl Thomas, and his wife Irene, pastored at the time of the fire. The fire marshal reported to him that an electrical short towards the front of the sanctuary had ignited the fire. For the record, Pastor Thomas stayed on and helped build the UB church on M-50, on the northside of the road just shortly before Highway 69.

If there was any good news, the Charlotte Seventh-day Adventist

Church, located in the 400 block of South Sheldon, the first place north of where my folks lived way back in the early 30s, offered us the SDA church the following Sunday and from then on until the new church was built. I believe it was Dr. Lester Sevener who gave this invitation. As a side note, the Clements trio (my mother, my sister, and myself), were asked for music on the first Sunday. The song we sang was, "I'll Trust in Him, Though I Don't Understand."

My future wife, Donna Jean Batdorff, and I were scheduled to be married in June at the old church. Obviously, this was not going to happen now, so we rented the Charlotte Free Methodist Church (at that time) close to Fulton Lumber Company on North Washington Street, as we needed a large church for our wedding. Originally, Donna's grandfather, Rev. J.I. Batdorff, was going to marry us, but because of his poor health, we had to get another pastor. My mother suggested her uncle Dr. George Fleming, who was a missionary for about 35 years in Sierra Leone, Africa. On June 18, 1955, I married the love of my life, Donnie. Sadly, only about two months after our wedding, Donna's grandfather did pass away on September 6, 1955.

The bottom line is that it was very sad to lose our old church, but when you consider the outcome and the new church which gave us more room and added congregation, I guess all things are still in the Lord's plan. Sometimes we just need to "step back" and watch the Lord work things out. He knows the end from the beginning; we don't.

Chapter Seventeen
CAREFREE AND WINTER JOBS

We haven't said much about my major job because most of this book is covering other areas. I worked at Carefree for nearly 39 years. In one sense, you could say it was part of the American Dream. I started with a very small new company and saw it grow over the years while I, in turn, moved up the corporate ladder. The job started at Carefree (then called General Aluminum Products, for the first few years) in March of 1956. When I started, the company was only three or four months old. There were five in the plant and two in the office producing aluminum storm windows. The company started in Eaton Rapids, Michigan and stayed there until February of 1960 (about three and a half years). About the time when the company moved to our much larger facility in Charlotte, is when we changed the name to Carefree. Over the years in Charlotte, we added onto the original facility at least five times. At that time, when we already had three children (family of five), for forty hours, my take home pay was less than $40. With my wife taking care of our ever-growing family, I needed part time jobs to keep the family afloat.

In the late spring of 1958 and 1959, I worked for Gulliver's Hatchery in Eaton Rapids. Chuck Gulliver and his brother worked not only in the Hatchery (where they raised baby chicks and sold them to local farmers), but they also had their own second enterprise in Ithaca, by Saint Louis, Michigan. They had six or seven very large chicken coops where they would raise about 10,000 young hens per coop. The chickens would remain there until the time when they started laying eggs; they would then sell them to farmers who wanted to start with mature laying hens.

There is a problem, however, with that large of a group of young hens. If, for any reason, there is a spot of blood that shows up on one of the chickens, the others would attack each other and could easily kill off many of the young hens. For this reason, when the chicks were about half grown, two or three pounds each, we four chicken "catchers," would go in one large van with the two Gulliver's to begin the debeaking process. This had to be accomplished well after dark to keep the chickens calm until you catch them and debeak each bird, one at a time. This debeaking takes about a quarter-inch off the top beak. The process is called "cut and cauterize." The machines to do this were manned by the Gulliver brothers.

To make this happen, we would arrive on those late spring evenings at least an hour after dark when the chickens were all settled down. We would put a divider across the center of the coop after we had carefully shooed the chickens to one end. That means that each of us catchers had to pick up about four to six chickens at a time, slowly, cautiously, and carefully to take them to the debeakers (the two Gulliver brothers). The process would take close to three hours to do the 10,000 chickens. Not hard to figure that each catcher, per night, had to catch 2,500 birds each, and carefully put them in the half of the coop that had been closed off for the birds that had been debeaked. Then, of course, we headed back home to Eaton Rapids.

We did this process either once or twice a week until all seven coops had been debeaked. For this very hot, yes, stinky job, we were paid a whopping $10 flat a night. I got about two or three hours of sleep before I had to get back up to go to work.

One of the other part-time jobs that I will explain to you, was with a company in Charlotte named Willcox-Gay. This company had been around for some time, making large radios, recorders, as well as prime parts for other like manufacturers. This was in the early 50s before I was married, and before TV had made a true foothold. Though there were TVs around, it is safe to say less than half of the homes had one. There were about 30 of us that were hired for the second shift, from 3 p.m. to 11:30 p.m., allowing for the half-hour lunch. Little did I know that the company had been fighting with the union and it was a difficult task when they were already in a shrinking industry.

The first afternoon, I was brought a large 55-gallon drum filled with parts that were bent improperly and needed to be straightened out. I found out later, that because these were small parts, a drum of this material would take most people more than an eight-hour shift to empty the barrel. I completed the first barrel in under six hours. I advised the foreman that I needed more parts; he looked surprised, but said nothing and brought me another barrel. The next day when I showed up to work, the union foreman met me at the door and advised me that if I kept working that hard, I would be sorry. With the work ethic that my dad and grandfather had given me, I couldn't believe what I was told.

The end of the story goes like this. On the 30th day of working the new job, the company foreman called us all together about 10:45 in the evening to advise us that we were all being laid off that night (at 11:30 p.m.). Only two of us, myself, and a friend of mine named Charley, went back to work to finish our job. We were harassed, but I simply said, "I was hired to work until the end of the shift, and that is what I'm doing."

Now back to Carefree. As I indicated, by February of 1960, we moved into Charlotte to our new location. I had already moved up to "head" of the picture window department, and from there to my next job as foreman of the storm window line. In another chapter, I mentioned that Stan Haigh was a good friend and competitor in the 4H area. He was now my main saw person cutting all the parts for the windows. There were ten people on the line and we had an excellent crew working together, setting records almost weekly in the amount of completed storm windows we were getting per day.

After the window department, I became the purchasing director of the company, and from there I became general manager of the company for the last 18 to 20 years before I retired. Along with being the general manager, one of my duties was to join AAMA (American Aluminum Manufacturers Association). For the record, though the acronyms stayed intact, the name was changed slightly over the years to incorporate all structures of windows, such as wood, aluminum, steel, and composite. The name was changed to American Architectural Manufacturers Association. In the first few years of my joining, I became vice president of the storm window and door division, and later worked with well in excess of 3,000 manufactures, setting the national window standards.

An interesting thing happened about this same period of time because I was general manager and heavily involved with sales. Our president, Richard Trumley, asked me to go with him to a new larger account he wanted to try to secure in Wisconsin. I believe the trip was successful in achieving our goal. We had flown from Lansing through O'Hare in Chicago, to our destination in Wisconsin.

We just started our return flight from central Wisconsin, when the pilot came on the speaker and said that there seemed to be a severe problem with the steering and landing gear, and he couldn't tell by the instrument panel whether the landing gear was locked in place up or down. For the record, we were flying on a Convair 580. With two large engines, the plane only seated 48 people, two on each side of the aisle and 12 rows deep. Back to the story. The pilot had another plane fly by us, who told us the wheels were down, but could not tell if the wheels were locked in place or not. At that juncture, he quickly told us to take our glasses off, put them in our pockets, fold our arms, and lay our heads on the seat in front of us, to prepare for a belly crash landing.

I immediately prayed and told the Good Lord it was all up to Him. If this was my time, I was ready. In the next 30 seconds to one minute, I just thanked Him for salvation, my good wife, and our kids, turned them all over to Him and felt an inner peace like I've never felt before or since. The peace was so comforting I almost felt giddy, my dumb sense of humor took over. I told Dick, my president, "You know, on most of these air crashes, if anyone survives, they are in the back of the plane. We were in the second row to the front." Then I said, "You see those large seven-foot propellers? We will probably be wearing them shortly!" For some reason, Dick said, "Will you shut-up!?" Oh, I forgot to tell you, Dicks verbiage was very different from mine, yet for some reason, I respected him, and he knew I would not lie to him. And it appeared that he had the same respect for me.

The problem with the wheels (landing gear) was all in the instrument panels. The pilot set that plane down so gently that it wouldn't damage a pea. The next day our vice president of finance, who was a friend of Dick's, had talked to him and then came into my office, closed the door, and told me that Dick said, "I don't know what Harold's got, but I can tell you, it's real!"

Before we close this area, I want to go back to an earlier time when I was still director of purchasing. I was going to a supplier that was north of Kalamazoo and running late. I had a dumb idea that going cross-country would be faster. As usual, I was wrong.

Coming in to a very small village, I was right behind a semi. The road appeared to be clear ahead, so I started to go around the semi, when I had a very strong feeling *don't pass*. I couldn't see anything and thought it was unusual, but I still dropped back of the semi for roughly a mile. The second time, I pulled out again and everything seemed okay, so I passed the semi. Looking ahead I saw a very large curve going out of this village with guard rails on either side of this two-lane road. Less than a block ahead a woman had taken the curve too fast, had lost control and was sliding sideways towards me taking up both lanes.

Then it hit me, if I had been around the truck on the first pull, there would have been no place for me to go. I simply pulled my car over to the side of the road and thanked the Good Lord one more time, for sending guardian angels or whatever He did, and thanked Him for giving me traveling mercies one more time, that I did not deserve. Although I was a few minutes late, the meeting went well, and one more time the Good Lord had reasons to keep me alive.

P.S. A very elderly woman, let's say late 80s, had just gotten on a plane; she had the Bible in her lap and appeared to be extremely nervous (probably her first flight). A young man sat down beside her and couldn't help but notice that she was nervous. He, also being a Christian, said, "Ma'am, you don't have to worry! Jesus said, 'I am with you always, even until the end of the age.'" The elderly woman smiled and said, "Young man, you are not quite right. What the Good Book really said was *"Low,* I am with you always." I guess the message was understood from both sides. For the record, my dad said he wouldn't mind flying if he could figure out how to keep one foot on the ground.

Chapter Eighteen
WASHINGTON D.C. OR BUST

I n the spring of 1967, we decided as a family to take a short vacation to the nation's capital and visit the historic monuments and landmarks. With a family of seven, we had a very tight budget. It is hard to believe, but we took a five-day vacation, and other than taking a few sandwiches and a tank of gas to get started, our total allowance for gas, hotels, meals, entertainment, and admission tickets, was a total of $160. Because of that almost impossible task, I gave my wife Donnie, $80 (half), and told her to hang on to it until I asked for it. Telling her that when we start on the last $80, we would have to start heading for home within a day and a half.

We visited all the popular places we could get into. The Capitol and Whitehouse happened to be closed on those few days. We did, however, see the Lincoln Memorial, walked all the way up in the Washington Monument to view the city from a higher viewpoint. We also visited a couple of museums like the Science Museum, and the Air and Space Museum, and spent time at Arlington National Cemetery, which at this writing, had over 400,000 markers of the brave men and women who gave their lives. This was very impressive even to our young family.

To show the difference of time, we were able to get motels for $6 or $7 a night, gas as approximately 30 cents a gallon, and we could get minimal meals for the entire family for $12-$15 a day. My, how times have changed! The most memorable part of the trip, however, was our trip to Mount Vernon to visit Washington's home. This stop was done late in our trip, with the hope to visit a few more places before we headed back. We did not arrive at Washington's home till midafternoon. We stopped at several places around the estate and, as usual, took pictures of the family around the garden, one at the house, and a few others. We did not leave the estate area until around 4:45 p.m., which was around closing time.

I had only gone roughly ten miles, when I said to Donnie, "Well I'm about out of money, give me the $80 that I gave you to keep for us." My wife almost turned blank, started looking for her purse, and couldn't find it. She thought she must have left it in the rose garden, which she set aside so it wouldn't be in the picture. By this time, I was panicking. Immediately I turned around and started heading back. When we got there, however, I was further shocked that they had already locked up. In those days, we did not have, and most people did not have, such things as credit cards. Remember when I asked for the money, I would already be broke. Now, what would we do?! We rattled the gate, did a little screaming and shouting, but nothing happened. Stupid though it was, I felt I had no choice but to follow the fence back nearly a quarter of a mile where I thought I could scale it, and started back towards George Washington's House. I was nearly there, when they caught me and started reading me the riot act. They also advised me that I was fortunate that the huge guard dogs had not torn my leg off by now. I strongly explained to them our predicament, the size of my family, and that we were over 600 miles from home with no money. What choice did I have, but to do what I did? Their answer was, "We don't care, you broke the law, you are going to pay for it." I finally, however, at least convinced them to look for my wife's purse in the rose garden. They searched, but could not find it. Did you think I was in trouble before? Now I was *really* in trouble and no one believed me.

Meanwhile, however, my wife remembered that was probably not where she left her purse. She went to the fence, saw a guard a hundred yards away, and tried to explain her story and get them to look in a couple of areas where she could have left it. When the guard came, though my story was getting thinner all the time, I put on my best sales hat and with much silent prayer, tried one more time. Somehow, with the help of the good Lord, I was able to try to convince them to try one more time, explaining that not only could I do nothing from jail, but that they would have the problem of trying to get my family home without any money. Again, I re-explained to them my story that I was completely broke without my wife's purse and the money. They finally agreed to go check one more time to the other two locations (VERY reluctantly). And thank God, they did find her purse. Their answer at this point was, "Fine, we'll let you go, but we are going to keep your wife's purse and the money and mail it to you." After firmly going through it one more time, they reluctantly conceded that though I had acted foolishly that my story did check out, and after one more stern lecture and raking over the coals, they did hand over the purse with the money. The good Lord had come through for us one more time.

Frankly, everything else was anticlimactic compared to that day. The kids, my wife, and I will never forget that visit or the day… What a nightmare. P.S. Remember, even though we make stupid choices, the good Lord will still help us when we *truly ask*.

Chapter Nineteen
GOD'S "SECOND" FIDDLE

Yes, you're right. That is an unusual title that stuck with me. You will find it is a logical title to explain my friend, Maurice Cherry, both in his life and in his passing.

Maurice's parents, Richard and Ruth Cherry, lived on North Cochran Road, in Charlotte, Michigan, about one block north of the railroad tracks on the west side, in a brick home. Maurice was the oldest son and was joined by three brothers, Harold, Howard, and Herbert. Interestingly enough, all three of Maurice's younger brothers were ministers. They pastored in the United Brethren of Christ Church, in Michigan, Ohio, and in Indiana. Herbert, the youngest was only about six months older than I, and one of my closest friends.

Now back to the story, Maurice was a very unusual individual. Most times with a quiet demeanor, and therefore quite "laid back" in his approach to life. He and his wife Rebecca, lived briefly on Maple Street in Charlotte, before moving to their farm home which was on the west side of Broadway, just over half a mile west of South Cochran, where Donna and I lived and raised our family. We lived on the southwest corner of South Cochran and West Broadway, which means Maurice and Rebecca lived about a half-mile west on Broadway on the south side of the road.

Before I get into that fateful day, and before I give you Maurice's life's work, let's tell you a little more about Maurice. Because of his "laid back" approach to life, he was many times slow or late. Underneath what would appear to be a very calm nature, he was mischievous and you never knew what he was going to come up with. The reason for the title, however, was because I never saw anyone in my lifetime that had less need to be number one. If someone was late or didn't show up to teach a Sunday school class, he would immediately step in without question. I was a song leader, but if for any reason I couldn't be there, I felt comfortable calling Maurice at the last minute to fill in, which he would do immediately with no argument. The same was true if anyone needed a Sunday School teacher, or help with the church (like repairs). You could always count on Maurice to fill the gap that would have otherwise been left void.

Back in those days, "bellings" were very common. That's where you tried to take a newly married couple by surprise, very late at night, usually at least midnight and lovingly demand the wife to bake pancakes or whatever else came to mind. Other things that happened would be like taking the new bride and groom into town and making him push her in a wheelbarrow down Mainstreet.

When Donnie and I were first married, we lived in a very small eight-by-nineteen-foot trailer, set in my folk's yard. Of course, it was Maurice who led a brigade of men with five chainsaws which were all started together and put up to our small trailer windows and literally smoked us out! On that July evening, it was probably still over 80 degrees, even after midnight. If there was any other odd thing, that could be thought up, Maurice would be the first in line to try it out. That is why I and others in the church waited for quite some time before "belling" Maurice and Rebecca, because they were, of course, watching for it, and we wanted to wait long enough to catch them "flat-footed." So, at least a year after they had moved to the farm, we had our opportunity. We did not get there till well after midnight, roused them up, and I can't remember all the mischief we caused, but for one thing, while we were keeping them "busy" downstairs, three or four of the men snuck upstairs, opened one of the windows, and put half of the furniture on the roof and then we left. You got it, we got even with him and some besides.

Now back to the story. Maurice and Rebecca had five children. The oldest was Linda, then Eric, Bonnie, Calvin, and the tag-along "Maurine." Just as a side note of interest, Bonnie, the middle child was only slightly older than Steven, our oldest, and she was kind of our "built-in" babysitter. She was very responsible, and we appreciated her so much that we even took her on two of our family vacations. One of these vacations was in Canada, where we were eaten up by gnats so much so that we came home early. The other was to northern Michigan to little Glen Lake, by Michigan's sand dunes. So, on top of being close to Maurice and Rebecca, we had special ties to Bonnie.

On the job front, most of Maurice's adult life was spent working for Consumers Power out of Lansing. He worked there until he retired only one month before his death. His second occupation was working for Wertz Implement Company, in Charlotte, selling milking machines and other supplies. His third job was farming, which he loved, and kept him more than busy. He promised his wife Rebecca that once he retired from Consumers, he would then take her on a nice long vacation, because with three jobs going, he didn't have time to work on a vacation.

Because of his natural nature and his three jobs, Maurice was always running behind on his farming. Whether it was putting in crops, cutting hay, or whatever, it seemed like he could not quite get caught up and basically it didn't seem to seriously bother him. His wife Rebecca was always busy, baking cakes for weddings, birthdays, funerals, or whatever, as that was her second job and she was a very good baker. She laughingly would say that the only time Maurice was "on time" was when it was time to eat. Therefore, on the day we are about to describe, when he didn't show up promptly at his six o'clock supper hour, she immediately became concerned.

Now the part I don't want to write, but must. On August 15, 1987, I was working in the garden when Donnie received a very urgent call from Rebecca. It was now between 6:15 and 6:20 p.m. and Maurice had not shown up. She had briefly checked the field where he was working, which was right near the house and barn (immediately west). She heard the machine still running, but after calling his name several times, there was no response. At that time, she told my wife, "Please, immediately send Harold down!" She told Donnie that she believed he was "gone" meaning that she thought that he was dead.

I jumped in the car, hurried down, and went directly to the field. I sprinted to the machine while calling "Maurice" at the top of my voice. With no response, and the machine now stalled out, I had no choice but to start to crawl underneath the machine. I won't describe what I saw, but I did get close enough to check his pulse, and there was no response.

In the meantime, either Rebecca or my wife had called the EMTs, ambulance, and firetruck, and they arrived approximately five minutes after I was there. They asked me what I knew, and at that point I still had no answers. I only knew that there was no way that I could lift that heavy machine off Maurice. With all the men together, they finally got the job done. At this time, there was an obvious reason why Maurice could not get away from the machine. The pickup tines that would normally lift the hay to go thought the hay conditioner had gone between his knee and his ligament and had bent him backward, pulling him under the machine giving him no possible way of escape.

After the EMT and other medical personnel had taken the body and left, I immediately started looking to find out if I could piece together what had happened. It was not too hard to spot when you consider that the machine on its own had been pulling Maurice for an estimated 15 to 30 minutes and was zig zagging all over the field. I could immediately tell that within 100 yards west of the barn the straight line had ceased. Close by, I found a stick three-quarter of an inch through and about two feet long with heavy scraping marks. What obviously happened was that the stick had gone under the belt, and went crossways into a pulley, causing the machine to stop. Why Maurice got out in front of the machine without turning it off or making sure the clutch was disengaged, we will never know. So, Maurice would have to have been in front of the machine when he leaned over and jerked the stick from out against the pulley. The clutch engaged immediately and started forward. As indicated earlier, with the tine inserted between the kneecap and ligament, the machine would have pushed Maurice backward, and there would have been no way of escape.

Within moments, friends, neighbors, children that were available (Linda and Eric were out of the area), everyone began to arrive. I must confess in my entire life I have never had to counsel three ministers back to back. So, between neighbors, children, friends from church, and others, I had to repeat the story many times over, explaining to the best of my ability what must have happened. I saved that stick for a couple of months until I finally decided (after many nightmares), it was time to dispose of it.

At the funeral, I was asked to speak, reciting some of the times I mentioned here, and called Maurice for the first time, "God's 'Second' Fiddle." I could not think of any better title that would fit Maurice than that. After the funeral, several of the young boys who had been in Maurice's Sunday school class came up to me and expressed what an impression he made on their lives. Maurice had the unique ability to be "one of them." That day, in August 1987, will never leave my mind. Maurice is resting in peace, sleeping till Jesus calls us home. What a man. What a Christian influence. What an example.

Question: What kind of vitamin should a Christian take?
Answer: B1. In other words, just *be one*!

Chapter Twenty
FALLON'S STORY - A LITTLE CHILD...

Our nicest home was our home on East Santee, nearly eight miles north of Charlotte (seven miles north, one mile east). The home was located on the southside of the road. We purchased the thirty-acre area with a beautiful brick home on a slightly elevated plateau. There was a creek that ran across the front, which our granddaughter Kari Nicole (Clements) Morrison, named Brook Cherith. This naming was accomplished when she was only about eight or nine years old. I was impressed that, as a young child, she was already applying spiritual things. She named it because the brook went dry two or three months (like July and August) every year and this reminded her of the story of Elijah. The woods surrounding the home had at least 200 sugar maple trees, some large oaks, beeches, and other varieties. We had trails, at least four or five, mostly running east to west through the woods, with one smaller trail headed just back of the woods for our brush pile.

My job was to play the adult version of pick-up-sticks so that our four-wheeler (a Yamaha), could travel smoothly when taking the grandkids for rides. To pick up the sticks, I would take many of the grandchildren (one at a time) and let them steer the Yamaha in idle gear. I instructed them to never touch the gas feed, and it would crawl along less than a mile an hour while I ran around picking up the sticks and putting them in the John Deere trailer that held about fifteen bushels. Even though the grandkids were very young, in Fallon's case only three or four years old, they minded very well and only did the steering. We would take the small trail once the trailer was loaded, and unload the sticks on our brush pile till it got about six feet tall. Then we would invite all the grandkids (who were available) for a bonfire of roasted marshmallows, smores, hotdogs (mostly vegetarian), singing songs, and mainly having a good time.

One afternoon, while heading the last 200 yards towards the brush pile, Fally looked back and said, "Grandpa, a wheel came off the trailer!" We stopped, but let me explain. Looking for the parts is not as easy as you would think because this smaller trail used less often, had knee-high grass, weeds, and small sticks, so the only things easy to find were the wheel and the hubcap. Fallon and I diligently searched for at least twenty minutes and could not find two items, the washer that fit over the spindle and a small cotter key that held it in place. Exhausted, Fallon, with the look of childlike innocent faith said, "*But, Grandpa we haven't prayed yet.*" We both dropped to our knees and simply said, "Jesus, Fallon and I need Your help. You know where those small parts are; we obviously don't have a clue. Please help us find them." We went back over the tall grass and ground where we had already searched and within one minute, sure enough, both parts were found.

No wonder the Bible says in Isaiah 11:6, "A little child shall lead them." How simple, yet what profound answers Grandpa received that day. No wonder the Good Book says, "Pray without ceasing" (1 Thessalonians 5:17), and "Be anxious for nothing, but in everything by prayer and supplication, with thanksgiving, let your requests be made known to God" (Philippians 4:6). Remember prayer is not the last resort, prayer is the first option.

Chapter Twenty-one
800 EAST SANTEE - A GRANDKIDS PARADISE

One evening, my wife and I were just looking through the countryside, looking for a wooded area to entertain the grandkids as they were growing up. Our realtor said, "Take a quick glance at this, but you may find it more expensive than what you want to pay." When I pulled into the drive, my good wife took one look and said, "This is it!" It was set on 30 acres with mostly woods of 200 or more hard maple trees, many large beech trees, and large red oaks. The house was elevated up a sloping drive about 150 yards off the road. It was a beautiful brick home with a very large garage, and a very gorgeous setting. There was a small creek not more than 60 or 70 feet off the road that ran across the property. As mentioned previously, this creek was named Brook Cherith by our granddaughter Kari.

I asked the grandkids to help supply me with some of the things that they remembered from the 14 years we lived at the property. Not in perfect order, but here they are. Fallon and two or three of the others mentioned Grandma and Grandpa hunting for morel mushrooms, taking them to the house, Grandpa frying them in pure butter and just a hint of flour, seasoned with salt, pepper, a hint of garlic, Mrs. Dash "Table Blend", and "veggie herb season." I must tell you, there is nothing better than that!

When Austin and Adam were young (our two youngest grandsons), less than two for Austin and Adam about four years of age, I showed them something very special. The woods were filled with deer and tons of wild turkeys. I had just come through the far edge of the woods from the west and almost stumbled on a baby fawn that had just been born. It was still wet. Austin happened to be with us that day (I think Grandma was babysitting), so I carefully tiptoed him out to the spot. This mother deer had hidden the baby fawn so well camouflaged that you had to be within three or four feet to spot this newborn beauty. I then went back and got Adam from his place so he could see this young fawn. You couldn't help but marvel at how the mother deer was trying to let us know that we were trespassing. She stood not more than 30 or 40 feet away pawing the ground and snorting to let us know we better get out of there. I can't believe we were so fortunate that this incredible little ball was still wet from birth when we first saw it. How blessed can we be!

As I indicated in Fallon's story, we took all the grandchildren with me riding on our 4-wheeler (Yamaha). We would take them on several trails (we had about six), and one key spot was a steep short hill right close to Brook Cherith that dropped off six or seven feet in not more than fifteen feet. I would hit this at nearly 35mph, while they screamed as I tried to change our direction quickly enough to not end up in the creek. While we were doing this, the rest of the grandchildren were on our 12-foot rectangular trampoline up close to the house. They would rate who was screaming the loudest to win the invisible prize. While on that point, when you have 200 maple trees in the area, raking leaves could be fun, but a big pain. I had a pile of leaves, no more than three or four feet tall, next to the trampoline. Led by Jenna, the grandkids plowed into that pile of

leaves screaming at the top of their lungs. I admit I was slightly upset, however, I cannot help but laugh now when I think of all the fun they had wrecking what I was trying to accomplish.

On the east side of our house, we had a porch that came off the top deck about eight feet wide and ran about 30 feet down the east side of the house. Four or five steps down off this deck, I had built a large gazebo that had a very large hot tub. From this level, if you went again another four or five steps down you would be at the walk-in basement level. Interesting to note, this home had three nine-foot patio doors on this side, two of the three opened to the 30-foot deck and the third one into the walk-in level. All the children

enjoyed the hot tub and Grandma did too because the lower level was not carpeted in the 9-foot patio door area downstairs. She would just laugh, give them a towel to dry them off and send them to the lower bathroom to change their clothes.

I can't help but throw in here that our second son Scott, always looking for something different, had come with his family from Florida around Christmas time. To their liking, that evening we received in excess of six inches of snow, while the evening temperature dropped to about 25 degrees Fahrenheit. As only Scott would do it, he sat in the hot tub just long enough for him to get acclimated, jumped out, rolled in the snow (like you would expect a Floridian to do), and got back into the hot tub. My wife and I, being from the north, wouldn't do this ourselves, but it was funny to see him dive into the snow and right back into the hot tub.

The inside of our home featured two sunken living rooms, one upstairs, one down. The upstairs living room featured four very large, angled, tapered glass windows totaling 16 feet wide and the glass was 92 inches tall from knee-high level to the peak. There were two fireplaces (doubled) on both the upper and lower levels. The best feature was that you could enjoy the four-foot deep fireplace from either side, the living room side, or the dining room side (when upstairs). Before I go downstairs and describe that, we must note that out our front large windows stood a huge oak tree that had a den of coons. Grandma Donna, at different times, would look out these large windows towards the road and often there would be a coon crawled halfway up the petitions between the windows and just look through the window like he was spying on my wife. Those memories will always linger. The fireplaces had a different facing on each one. The prettiest one was downstairs in the sunken living room which featured cut fieldstone, the other side was white brick. The upstairs had brick the same color as the outside of the house.

Downstairs featured a spiral staircase from top to bottom. We had to really watch the grandkids because they very much enjoyed this staircase! We had to make certain that they were safe! When Kari was about three or four (when we first bought the place), she slipped going down, and luckily, I was down below to catch her! She could have really gotten hurt, because in that section of that lower walk-in, it was all cemented and the carpet didn't start until the sunken living room. Downstairs we also had a partial kitchen for all the families to bring in their potluck, which we put on the tennis table so everyone could enjoy a very generous  helping of whatever was their favorite. At the far end of the basement (the west end) was a large 13 by 26-foot room with a pool table. This was a center of attraction for all those who wanted to play pool.

When Grandma was younger, as we all were at one time, she would start chasing the grandkids around the pool table and/or the tennis table, going upstairs and down. For this she was endeared the title of "Mad Grandma." I, on the other hand, put the young ones on my shoulders and was having fun doing the same thing that "Mad Grandma" was doing, chasing the kids. Only, I had someone on my shoulders to boot!

One thing my wife and I have always remembered is that our daughter Mindy and her family had moved into a new home on the east side of ours. Between us and them was a fairly steep short hill with lots of undergrowth of trees and a path that led between their house and ours. Donnie and I had been over to their place late one evening and asked Adam, who was now roughly three years old, if he would like to go to breakfast with Grandma and me, *sometime.* Sure enough, 7:30 the next morning the garage doorbell rang, and here was Adam ready for his breakfast. Grandma said, "Adam, do your parents know you are here?" He just hung his head which simply meant… "No" … Not knowing exactly how to handle this, we loaded him in the car, drove around to their driveway only to find out that they didn't have a clue that he had slipped out of the house, came through woods by himself, and decided that *today was the day*! Adam almost did not get to go to breakfast that day, as his dad and mother were very upset that he had snuck out of the house without their permission. Right or wrong, I tried to convince his dad, Craig, that we were alright with it, but that obviously Adam needed a serious talking to because of his age. The fifth commandment clearly states, "Honor your father and your mother, that your days may be long upon the land which the Lord your God is giving you" (Exodus 20:12). Adam's disobedience nearly cost him his breakfast and a very firm loving correction. Note that this is the only commandment that carries a promise of long life. Somehow, we have lost an awful lot of respect for parents, grandparents, great grandparents, neighbors, teachers, and so forth in the last 100 years. We all need to do our part to get this commandment restored. What a beautiful home and location; what memories of the grandchildren we had.

Our Grandkids on the Front Porch

Chapter Twenty-two

LAUGH, INSTRUCT, DISCIPLINE, AND FAMILY TIMES

SECTION ONE: LAUGH

While still attending the Charlotte UB Church, the Sunday School classes would often hold monthly meetings. The reasons were for good social times, of reading Scripture, having prayer, and singing a couple of songs before having *light* refreshments (Pun: They served it on a lamp, ha!). Many times, parlor games would follow.

One time, at my folk's house, we had one of these monthly meetings (this group was between 40-55 years old), they were singing the well-known hymn "Leaning on the Everlasting Arms." Let me set the stage. I had two or three aunts, who, let's say, were a little plump. Halfway through the chorus, as they were singing, "safe and secure from all alarm," my aunt's chair shattered in a hundred pieces, dumping her on the floor! After everyone found out that nothing was hurt, except her pride, the place broke out with hilarious laughter more than you've ever heard in your life! The old statement goes, "sometimes, even the angels laughed." At that moment, Heaven must have been an unusual scene. Just think, singing "safe and secure from all alarm," and then BAM! What perfect timing! I must admit I thought some of the ladies would never again regain composure.

SECTION TWO: INSTRUCT

I am not always well organized. We had our large garden on South Cochran and you could not always find the tools in our shed. Hoes, shovels, water hoses, or anything used for gardening never seemed to find their place. If I wanted a hoe it could take ten minutes to find it! So, I asked son number three, Simeon (Sim, for short), "Would you please organize the shed?" Frankly, he did an excellent job. Not only did he take his job seriously, but from then on everything had its "home," making it easier for all of us while we were gardening. But just as a side note, guess whose garage is the most organized today? Oh, that would be Sim's! So, obviously, these minor habits have become standard to him and anyone who practices organization.

SECTION THREE: DISCIPLINE

The third area is about our second son, Scott, who required more discipline than the rest. He was just more curious than the others, and also seemed to challenge authority. He always would say, "It's not me" or "It's not my fault."

To set the stage, we had a part of our barn where we kept the horses and our pony, Ginger. It was Scott's job to water and feed them each morning. The 32-inch door leading into this area swung into the pen, with a screen door type spring attached to keep the door closed. When closed, we had a six-inch catch that locked down into a staple to secure the door. Our pony, Ginger, was smart enough that, if the catch was not latched, she would bump the door with her head, and get it bouncing wide enough so she could then walk outside.

On a cold blustery day in February, I received a call at work from my wife telling me the pony was in the neighbor's field and that I needed to come home and put her back in the barn. I came home, suit, tie, and all and put on heavy knee boots. The crusted snow was knee-deep, and although I *thought I was in good shape*, I quickly found out I was not! Every time I would take a step toward the pony, that elusive Ginger would move just far enough away that I couldn't get a hold of her. I honestly thought I was going to have a serious heart attack. It was over a half an hour before I finally got ahold of Ginger. I put her back in her pen, and, I must admit, the more I thought about it, the more I became upset! The exhaustion I felt was immense.

Needless to say, the discipline that I administered that night to Scott was more than usual. He kept saying, like normal, "I didn't do it!" -- Well frankly, I've heard that story before. *But* the story does not end there. About two days later it suddenly dawned on me, *I was the last one in the barn that morning.* Now, what do I do?! I could just tell myself, *well, that would balance all the other times he has lied or at least claimed to be innocent.* Regardless, that night I took Scott aside and profusely apologized to him. I admitted that I was wrong. I made a serious mistake. Is there any way he could forgive me?

Sometimes a bad situation can end up alright. Scott, who I think was twelve at the time, saw that Dad could admit when he was wrong, and we don't need to be ashamed to admit it. Frankly, from that time on, Scott and my relationship seemed to improve. It has appeared to be a turning point, both for Scott and for myself. Remember, discipline is needed, but it is how we react in love that is truly the only thing that matters. Proverbs 23:13-14 speaks that we should not spare discipline but lovingly administer it when needed.

SECTION FOUR: FAMILY TIME

Now let's cover some of my wife's and my musical background. In my wife's case, her mother, Madeline, would take the children to the piano and practice new songs two or three nights a week, so the Batdorff Trio would be ready on demand when called. On the lead was Joyce, my wife's next oldest sister. On tenor, was Howard Jr., and my wife was on the alto. They sang songs like, "Only One Life to Offer," which was not matched by anyone else. No one could do it as they did. I can still hear the balance of harmonies in memories recalled today.

Ours was similar in my family, except my mother played guitar and sang the alto. My sister, Wilma, sang the lead (melody), and

I was on tenor. My mother's favorite song was "My Savior," and probably our best-known song was "Hallelujah, to the Lamb." With that background, it was natural for us when our children were growing up, on South Cochran in Charlotte, or the grandchildren, later in our home on Santee, to always be singing.

How blessed my wife and I are, not only with her mother and my mother giving us the training we had, but for us to do the same thing in instructing our children and later our grandchildren to sing in four or five-part harmony. Whether that would be around a bonfire at sunset, the opening or closing of the Sabbath day, or around the piano as night draws near, we would sing,

> "Now the day is over, night is drawing nigh
> Shadows of the evening steal across the sky
> Father gives the weary, calm, and sweet repose
> With Thy tenderest blessings may our eyelids close."
> (Words by Sabine Baring-Gould in 1867)

And then a very warm *amen* which would wrap around you like a blanket on a cool winter's evening in Christian love and we could honestly say, "Hallelujah, what a Savior! Amen." The four or five-part harmony we were able to achieve would just make a beautiful opening or closing to the Sabbath day. What peace, what joy, what profound oneness in Jesus. PTL.

Chapter Twenty-three
SINGING WE GO - UNTIL THEN

The old saying is, "The family that prays together, stays together." I'm suggesting that the family that sings God's praises together, also bonds together. In this chapter, we are going to attempt to cover four generations. In an earlier chapter that ends up with family times, we have covered that both my wife's family and my family were taught by our mothers, hers around the piano, and mine was with my mother's guitar. Before we go into generation two, there is one other point that should be covered.

Donna's mother always loved music but, before she started going with Donna's father, all her joy of music came from music outside of the church and she enjoyed dancing. When she started getting serious with my father-in-law, they went to several services, where her future father-in-law, Rev. J. I Batdorff, was conducting the service. She was converted at that time. Madeline's father was a high Mason, and he was upset with the preaching because the UB's at that time were fairly strong in their teachings against the Masonic lodge (because they were a secret order). He was so mad that he kicked his daughter Madeline (Donna's mother) out of the home when she was about 17 or 18 years old. A doctor friend of hers felt sorry enough for her and the situation, that he invited her to stay with them until she was married to Howard (my father-in-law). At that juncture of the street, her mother's interest immediately turned to gospel music, and that is where the teaching of Donna and her siblings originated.

In my family, our mother would pick the notes out on the piano and then convert it into the proper chords that would match the needed pitch for our voices. Other than that, where Donna's mother prepared them in advance, we only scrambled and worked hard to get a song once we were asked. With that said, we have now completed generation one.

Now generation two, which would be our combined family. We started teaching our children at a very young age, setting them down at the piano with us and basically following the pattern that her mother and mine used in teaching. Steven and Scott started, and the other children as they came along followed the same pattern.

When Steven and Scott were not more than four or five, we were already teaching them the melody. By the time they were six or seven, Steve had already started his training in singing tenor, and very shortly after Scott was singing alto with his mother. This is where the Clements family started singing, which would be in the mid-1960s. we would add Steven on the tenor, while Donnie and Scott were singing alto, and to make a trio, I moved over to the lead melody.

Over the years, as Sim, Mike, and Mindy were coming along, we would train them together (at start) to listen first to each other so that they were all on the same note. Steve and Scott started carrying their parts very well to make a good trio sound. At that juncture of the street, there was nothing left for Dad to sing, except bass. We were already heavily singing as a family by 1968. Both Donnie and I agreed that we would like to cut an album but with a family of seven, the three-thousand or more dollars needed were hard to come by. By 1969, and early 1970, I did decide to take the leap of faith, borrow money, and go to work! Our first endeavors were to contact Phase 8 studios in Kalamazoo, Michigan, and they agreed to record our singing. At the same time, I had asked Mary Esther (King) Batdorff to be our pianist just as she was for me in my earlier years (See chapter: General Conference - Harrisburg, Pennsylvania). My wife and I had also been singing trios quite regularly with a woman named Eva Booth out of Mio, Michigan, who had a good Seventh-day Adventist background and who could play the piano and sing. With our team now set, we scheduled in late 1969 or early 1970 to start recording with Phase 8.

The Album Cover of "Just a Closer Walk"

During the same period of time, we were very heavily involved in, not only the United Brethren church and other conservative denominations, but were also singing in the SDA churches. So, on Friday evening at sundown (Sabbath beginning) we started singing in the SDA church, and continued singing in the other churches until Sunday evening. Frankly, we were singing a minimum of two weekends per month and sometimes three. According to my records, it is estimated that we sang in 27 different variations that could be anything from Baptist, Nazarene, Methodist, Wesleyan Methodist, and all other conservative churches. To make the program complete, I would give a short devotional or, in some cases, give an abbreviated sermon. Many times I would also quote poems I had memorized.

Back to the recording. To control the cost, I did all the editing of our singing (which proved to be a mistake in a couple of areas because I missed a few bad notes!). Then we contacted Queen City Album Inc. in Cincinnati, Ohio, made arrangements for the money, and turned it over to them in mid-to-late 1970. Frankly, even in our own family, there is a slight disagreement as to when we finally received the albums, but it was somewhere in mid-1971, according to my records. We were promoting the sales, asking $5 per album. Happily, by mid-1973, we had enough to pay off our indebtedness. Praise the Lord!

One of the occasions that my family enjoyed was singing for the SDA Campmeetings in Grand Ledge, Michigan. For several years, during the 1970s, we had the privilege of presenting 20-30 minutes of music before very large crowds, just before the King's Heralds sang, which were part of the Voice of Prophecy Radio Program out of California. The speaker was Elder H.M.S Richards, the president of Voice of Prophecy. As a side note, Voice of Prophecy is one of the oldest radio stations in the United States, starting in 1925.

For the bicentennial of the signing of the Declaration of Independence (the original signing was in 1776), I was asked to conduct a large Charlotte area choir doing patriotic numbers and some old hymns like the "Battle Hymn of the Republic" in July of 1976. The choir was in excess of 75 members that came from 12 to 14 area churches. We sang at the courthouse lawn on July 4, and a special concert at the high school gymnasium which held more than 1,000 people. Both concerts were extremely well attended.

All five of our children attended Grand Ledge Academy for all four years of high school. Each of them started breaking off on their own in music after academy days. In some cases, our children were singing with the Clements' family, but they were also joining up with other groups. I will highlight each of the five children, their individual accomplishments, and how generation two of singing, led to generation three.

With Steven, the oldest, while still in academy was singing quartet with our son Scott, along with Ray Hilton and the music director Martin Sotala. There are times that Russ Durham filled in and you'll be hearing his name later as well. Steve's four years of college were at Andrews University in Berrien Springs, Michigan. There he sang with the university quartet where the voice teacher Dr. James Hanson, and Roy Lucman sang together. As you will see with Scott, the second son, also sang in this group in Steve's sophomore year. After Steve graduated from Andrews, he started his business career in the field of Medical Technology, which included blood lab testing and hematology, included blood counts and cancer cell research. At this juncture of the street, he lived in the Hinsdale, Illinois area, where he sang with the *Hinsdale Men's Chorus* which was about 35 men strong, and sang in a large metropolitan chorale which covered most of the small outlining areas west of Chicago, about 50 voices. We would be remiss if we didn't mention that all the children, during their academy days, were also singing in church choirs, chorales, ensembles, and more. One last note on Steve, after he and June (his wife), moved from Hinsdale, IL, to Marshfield, Wisconsin, he spent the balance of his business career at the Marshfield Clinic, one of the largest in the state of Wisconsin. While there, he was head-elder, in a small country church about eight miles outside of Marshfield. He did solos but also sang with his daughters, Stacy, Shelly, and Katie, on numerous occasions.

Our second son, Scott, said his first recollection of his musical journey started in the Sunday school of the UB church. His teacher seemed to get a little upset when at five or six years old, Scott said, "I want to sing the harmony part!" She asked him, "How did you learn to sing harmony?" He said, "I just hear it, doesn't everyone?" She didn't appear to like his answer. Scott indicated that at this time, to the best of his knowledge, his mother Donna, was becoming a Seventh-day Adventist. He also reminded me that six or seven years after we put together the album ("Just a Closer Walk"), we recorded another tape ("More Love to Thee") of the Clements' Family, at the Lansing SDA Church in Lansing, Michigan. As I was reviewing it, I noticed that our now-grown children, with quite a large voice range, would sing different parts on different songs. In other words, Scott sang mostly the first tenor but also sang on different songs: second tenor, baritone, and even bass. The same could be said of all the boys.

In academy, both Steve and Scott played trombone. I mention here again Russ Durham, who was one of the best trombone players I have ever heard. He still plays to this day, and is still good! Before Steve left academy he was also singing in our family quartet: Scott on first tenor, Sim on second tenor, either Steve or Mike on baritone, and Dad on bass.

Back to Scott. He also sang in the Andrews University Quartet, with Steven, Dr. Hanson, and Roy Lucman. I mentioned early that Steve graduated from Andrews University, but Scott left after his sophomore year and went to Southern Missionary College in Collegedale, Tennessee. At Southern, he soon joined the *DieMeistersingers*, directed by Dr. Marvin Robertson. The group varied from 50-75 voices, depending on the year. This was one of Scott's favorite groups; it was like his lifelong brotherhood. They still have reunions every five years. That experience is still instilled in Scott: total love for men's gospel chorus music.

After college, Scott moved to Orlando, Florida where he entered a lifelong career in Cardiology. Not only did he work in the heart-cath tech area, but he also taught at the college level in the evenings for the last 15 years. While at Florida Hospital, he sang with the *Florida Hospital Chorus,* under Dr. Peter Matthews. He also sang with the Bach Festival Chorus on the platform of the Bob Carr Auditorium, for the debut concert of the Orlando Philharmonic Orchestra which performed the fourth movement of Beethoven's Ninth Symphony.

In 2001, Scott started attending the Markham Woods SDA Church. He soon discovered that they had a very active men's chorus. The president of the chorus, Fred Stevens, asked him to join, which he did! At that time, it was just known as the Markham Woods Chorus. Scott was asked to sing the lead first tenor and, at that time, he suggested the group be renamed to *Men of Markham Woods*. In 2019, Fred Stevens retired after 25 years as president of the group. Scott was then elected as the group's president, and he still serves today. The group celebrated its 25th anniversary last June. Guess who is the current music director today? Russ Durham! You've heard his name before. Small world!

Before I leave Scott, I will mention his two children. Both have good voices, and Andrew, his oldest, sings the first tenor, just like his dad. Both Andrew and Alisha (his daughter), sing in the 50-voice chorus of the Florida Hospital and they both have sung at different times in the very large *Epcot Chorus* in excess of 300 people. They have performed at programs for the 4th of July and other major holidays.

Now we are going to son three and four together because a lot of their efforts have been in the same area, especially in *Four for the Master* quartet. Sim started singing with an early version of the quartet back in 1990. Prior to Sim joining, the quartet had been comprised of Ron Silvernail, 1st tenor; Todd Sotala, 2nd tenor

(Martin Sotala's son); Martin Sotala, baritone; and Ray Hilton, bass. When Martin Sotala retired from teaching, he moved to the upper peninsula in Michigan to start a farm. It was at this time that he suggested to the rest of the group that Sim should replace him. This early version of the quartet sang only occasionally with most requests coming from the Grand Ledge SDA, Charlotte SDA, Charlotte United Brethren, or other local churches.

During that time the quartet was known as the "Grand Ledge Academy (GLA) Alumni Quartet." After the frequency and distances of concerts increased, it was suggested by Dad (Harold Clements) that they consider a name change of *Four for the Master*. This was quickly adopted even though they always kept the tie to their heritage with Grand Ledge Academy as part of their logo.

Mike Clements joined the quartet in early 1993, replacing Todd Sotala as 2nd tenor. This was due to Todd's request as he was not wanting to commit to the heavier travel schedule that had become the new norm. Two recordings were produced and sold over the years: "Our Tribute" and "O Be Joyful." A third recording was started but never fully completed, named "Reaching." However, many of the songs for that recording were used in concerts for several years following.

Four for the Master

Four for the Master traveled twice to 3ABN (Three Angels Broadcasting Network) in West Frankfort, Illinois which broadcasts worldwide. The first trip was on March 27, 1996, and the second November 9, 1998. Many songs from these two trips were used over the next several years on the Network's "Melodies from the Heart" program.

In May of 1995, the group traveled to Wisconsin for a weekend tour of three churches. In 1996, the first recording became available for the first time. On October 5, 1997, *Four for the Master* had the honor of singing with the *King's Heralds* in a concert at the Lansing Seventh-day Adventist Church in Lansing, Michigan. The songs they sang were: "Written in Red", "It is Well", and "The Lord is Coming."

They also sang for the live Worldwide Teleconference Worship Service broadcasted by 3ABN from the Battle Creek Tabernacle in Battle Creek, Michigan, in February 2000. This was hosted by the Michigan Conference of Seventh-day Adventists. In November of 2009, they had the honor of singing for Dad's baptism. They sang: "Sweet, Sweet Spirit", "O Be Joyful", "Reaching", "When Creation is at Peace", and "It is Well." Over the years the quartet had the privilege of singing for many campmeetings, evangelistic meetings, Women's Ministries retreats, and Michigan Men of Faith events. Sim also sang for over five years with the *Eternity Singers* and with the *Lansing Chorale* for four years. Mike also sang in the *Lansing Chorale*, along with a couple of other people from the Charlotte Seventh-day Adventist Church, including two of my grandchildren Kristopher Clements and his wife, Kalicia.

Our daughter Mindy also sang with Sim in the *Eternity Singers*. Sadly, their director Lindy Bartelson died of a heart attack while umpiring a softball game. It was sad for two reasons, because of his passing the group broke up, and the balance of harmony that this 15-voice group could achieve was excellent. Mindy also sang in the academy choir and in the academy trio as well as with the band.

All of Generation Two Singers

In the balance of what is now the third generation, we would be amiss if we didn't say that Grandpa and Grandma had the huge privilege of singing with the majority of grandchildren. We have sung duets, trios, and quartets with most of them, but I must also say that many of them have very fine solo voices. When you drop down to let's say, Sim's family, their daughter Kari has a very excellent solo voice as well as Mindy's two daughters Jenna and Fallon. Many of the grandchildren went to Great Lakes Adventist Academy in Edmore, Michigan. It is safe to say that almost all our grandchildren sang in SDA academy choirs and other musical groups. What a privilege it has been for us to see our grandchildren in Christian education.

With this said, we now move into generation four. You've heard me mention Kari, in two or three of the other chapters. Kari married Christopher (with a C) Morrison and they now have four children. The oldest one, Jett Matthew Morrison is now nine years old but has already sung in three states. He has sung in Colorado, Michigan, and Florida. His mother has carefully taught him how to hold his lead voice against his mother's alto. When you consider his age, Donna and I think this is very special.

Our Oldest Great Grandson Representing Generation Four

So back to the start. Just as praying families have the ability of staying together, please note that this is the fourth generation that is singing to the glory of God. The Psalms are replete with the numerous times it tells us to sing and to praise Him. From the 146 Psalm to the end of the book, all five chapters start and end with "Praise the Lord" (which means, this repeats ten times). So, in closing, praise the Lord!

P.S. The old saying is, "The grass is always greener on the other side of the fence." But frankly, I am here to tell you that when you get there, it is Astroturf. In other words, it is artificial. It just looks greener.

Chapter Twenty-four
DAD - SLOWING DOWN, GARDENING, AND WALNUT HARVESTING

After I quit farming, the large herd of dairy cows became a burden for my dad. Between my dad and myself, we had sold between one and two million pounds of Grade A milk to the Lansing Michigan Market. So, slowly the herd became smaller and Dad sold the balance of the cows and started raising beef cattle.

Dad and I would buy a truckload or two of the young beef that averaged between 300 and 400 pounds. Most of these were Angus, with some Herefords. Most of the calves were steers (not heifers) and were purchased out of the Kentucky and Tennessee areas. We could normally purchase them for around 30 cents a pound, feed them for ten to eleven months, and sell them again for their approximate rate at 30-32 cents a pound. In the meantime, of course, they had gained between 600 and 700 pounds, which means that the now fatted steer would be between 1,000 and 1,100 pounds. At that rate, we could make a decent profit on the beef.

One year, however, we could not find any young calves under 38 cents a pound. We "gambled" and bought a truckload anyway. When we sold these fatted prime steers all we could get was about 24 cents a pound. Although we got most of our money back, we would have made much more if we had just sold the corn and hay we fed them as a cash crop. But like the story of the navy beans, our dad just said, "Oh well, we've had all this fun that we would have missed if we hadn't have done all that we did." Again, Dad's attitude was simple: if the problems stayed in the field or at the barn, with God's help, we could handle it.

In our folks' senior years, Dad would plant in his garden at least two or three times more than he or mother could use. Just as a side pun, the old statement about gardening was, "You eat what you can, and what you can't, you *can*." Well, Mom kept the Ball quart jar company in business, but it was still far more than they could eat or can.

Most of the extra tomatoes, sweet corn, cucumbers, muskmelon (or cantaloupe if you prefer), would be given away to the neighbors, friends, church widows, and whoever could use them. As a side note, our dad would sometimes become almost upset if he brought you, for the second time in the same week, extra produce only to find you hadn't eaten up the first yet. One neighbor, Mark Friar really helped Dad in return. When winter came, because of my dad's heart problem, everyone told him, "Don't shovel the snow!" Mark would bring his tractor and snowplow and keep Dad's driveway clean, almost before the snow stopped falling.

The last area I want to share with the readers was that in the fall months Dad would pick up bushels of black Michigan walnuts. He would shuck them, wash them, and dry the walnut shells until they were ready to crack. I admit, my mother would get close to upset finding Dad had stored BUSHELS, like 50 or 60 of them, either on or near a register, both upstairs and down in the house. Extra bushels went to the basement until Dad could start cracking them when they were cured. Then Dad would start cracking the walnuts, pick out the meats, and literally give 90 percent of them away. At Christmas times, all of us kids and many of the grandkids received full quarts of black walnut meats, at no charge. This was Dad's evening chore all winter. I am not exaggerating to say that Dad gave away thousands and thousands of dollars' worth of black walnut meat. I can tell you; you haven't had good cookies until they are loaded with black walnut meats.

With all the emphasis that I had mentioned on Dad, it would be wrong not to mention that Mother helped in the hoeing, cooking, canning, shucking peas, and so much more! Even in their senior years both my mother and father kept busy. Let me remind you what Dad always reminded me, he would say, "Son, God did not put a head on your shoulders just to keep your backbone from unraveling." In other words, "Use your head!"

Chapter Twenty-five
OAKWOOD ESTATES

T wo years before I retired, Donna and I bought our winter home in Winter Haven, Florida, off Spirit Lake Road. Oakwood is a home-owned park with 430 double-wide homes. We spent 28 winters there and went through three tornados. Fortunately, two of the three brought very minor damages to our home. For example, a lost shutter, and minor damage to some windows. The third tornado caused severe damage to the park, ripping apart several of the homes. Many had torn off carports, Florida rooms, many roofs, sections of siding, and other damages. Again, we were fortunate enough that we only had about $1,500 worth of damage.

While at Oakwood, I participated in the Polk County Senior Olympics for many years. Though I competed in several events like Long Jump, Shot Put, walking the 5,000 meters, my main event would be in the sprints. I started this when I was about 65 years old (just a kid!), and quit when I was 77 years of age. The reason for quitting was simple: a woman approximately a year or two ahead of my quitting was texting while driving and drove through a stop sign at 60 mph. She hit me like a perfect T-bone, dead center of my door, totaling it out. She hit me so hard on the driver's side that it crushed my hips from the left to the right and damaged my right hip bad enough that I needed a total hip replacement. The evidence showed, because of no skid marks, that she never even touched the brakes. The airbags saved their lives (her and her passenger), and the seatbelts kept my grandson Austin and me from more severe injuries, even though my truck nearly rolled over. Austin said that he could count the blades of grass as they flew by his window before the truck finally righted itself back on its wheels. Because of this accident, the doctor said clearly, "You can walk, or you can jog, but no more of this top-speed-sprinting!" Now back to the story. In those 12 years, I was never beaten, with exception of the times I pulled my hamstring, which was two or three times. In those races, I ran the 100 *meters*, between 16.3 to 16.6 seconds, and the 50 *meters* in approximately 8.5 seconds. This is without any spikes or starting blocks; just stand up and go!

While in Florida, we had an excellent church family at the Seventh-day Adventist Church in Winter Haven. My wife and I were afforded the privilege of singing in many services. I was also given the opportunity to give the messages while the pastor was on vacation.

We made numerous friends at Oakwood Estates, our retirement community. We had between four and six ministers living in the park, at any given time. Therefore, we had early morning sunrise services every Resurrection Sunday, and the ministers would take turns delivering a powerful "He Is Risen" message. On Good Friday morning, March 25, 2005, I could not get back to sleep between 3-4 a.m. I kept thinking of all the people and situations that happened in the Bible as they were trying to make sure they got "rid" of Jesus.

For starters, Judas sold Him, the Roman soldiers captured him, and it went on through His burial. In an almost audible voice, I heard Jesus say, "Harold, put it in writing," therefore the poem "They Thought They Had Won" was written. Talking to the minister that was going to deliver the message that Resurrection Sunday, I showed him the poem, and immediately he wanted to include it in his message. The poem was used again, for the Easter Sunrise service April 4, 2010. All the attendants who wanted it (over 200 in attendance), were given a copy of the poem. We are including it here below. Just to recap, Judas sold Him, the soldiers seized Him, Pilot authorized the crucifixion, He was nailed to the cross, buried in a borrowed tomb, but, thank God that was not the end of the story! Jesus rose triumphantly. Hallelujah! What a Savior.

"They Thought They Had Won"
By Harold Clements
(Written Good Friday Morning, March 25, 2005)

They thought they had won when Judas
Accepted the bribe that day,
And sold my Lord and my Savior -
Thirty pieces of silver his pay.

They thought they had won as he led them
To the garden where Jesus went to pray;
When the Roman soldiers seized him,
They thought it His final day!

They thought they had won when they nailed Him
To the cross, 'tween earth and sky;
Jesus carried our sins to the hillside
Where He suffered, bled, and died!

They thought they had won as they laid Him
Within a cold, borrowed tomb;
And rolled a huge stone o'er the doorway.
It was done - they had sealed His doom!

But...after the cross, the grave, came Sunday,
And with the dawn's first ray
Jesus, God's Son, arose triumphant
On that great resurrection day!

At the Father's right hand, He is waiting,
He who is the world's best Friend;
With trumpet sound and victory shout,
For Jesus *is* coming again!!

Chapter Twenty-six

FROM UB TO SDA

Written by Donna Clements

Before I get into my story, I want to share a little about my background and that of my mother. My mother was short and very small framed and had difficulty in the delivery of her children. She was an only child for 14 years and then her brother, Clifford, was born. Uncle Cliff was probably my favorite uncle because he would come to visit us at Sunfield and spend lots of time playing with us kids. I had two brothers and two sisters and I was the third in line of the five siblings. I also had three brothers that my mother had lost before I was even able to meet them; they are currently buried between my mother and father at the Sunfield Cemetery. Being that my mother was raised with 14 years difference between her and her brother, she was not used to a large family, although the Batdorffs were known to have many children. However, she ended up being a mother of a large family herself.

After Harold and I got married, my mother was also there during the delivery of our oldest son, and she was extremely concerned because she also had a very similar problem. I lost my vitals. They had to do the lifesaving jumper cables to save my life. My son, Steven, weighed 9 pounds 4 ounces and I weighed only 95lbs before the pregnancy. My doctor was just out of medical school and I was his very first delivery patient. He was frustrated and didn't know what to do, so he had to call in another doctor. Thankfully, I responded immediately to the treatment that they did. Of course, my mother and father, the church, and a lot of friends were praying. I was thankful that God had spared my life, and that Steven could be raised by his birth mother. A friend of mine had died in childbirth, but her baby was saved (at the mother's choice instead of her own life), and the baby did have to be raised by another mother. This impacted me because I desperately wanted to raise my own children. Steven John Clements was my first-born son. This was my parents' (Howard and Madeline Batdorff) first born grandchild.

Let's fast forward about 12 years to the beginning of my struggle. I felt devastated and was seriously depressed, we had four young sons at the time, and this might sound a little unusual but I was in a struggle of my life and desperate for answers. I was losing my mother to breast cancer; she had lost her father who had suffered horribly (that was before we had the treatments we have today). His suffering was so horrible, mother decided that she would not seek any cancer treatment. She refused treatment because she had seen the effects of others' lives, and that if they cut, the cancer would probably just continue to spread on and on. At the time, there was little treatment that would help. She did some home treatments that she had studied about and it did help for nearly seven years. Finally, at my urging, she accepted some blood transfusions. We all knew that this would not save her life, but would make her more comfortable. Only a few weeks later she passed away at the age of 53 into the sleep of death. I also had lost a young cousin that I was very close to, he was only 30 years old. I lost an uncle in his 40s and an aunt at a very early age. I felt very close to this aunt. When I found out my mother had cancer, I figured that it must run in the family, because of all the other relatives (including her father, who died in his 40s from cancer).

I had so many fond memories with my mother. Three days a week in the evening we would practice music when I was young. She always had the desire that we would be a musical family. She played the piano for practice (but would never play in public). We would always sing acapella for the performance. I learned early on, with my brothers and sisters, how to sing trios. We would sing for quite a few churches in the United Brethren denomination. We were constantly learning new music even before we were called to sing. She always wanted us ready for when we were asked to sing again.

Mother and Dad were both very serious about having consistent family worship. They would even have us miss the school bus if we were running late: worship came first. Each of us were prayed for by both of our parents before we left for school. This was an important matter. I always knew that my parents had a true relationship with God and that I could trust their spiritual guidance. Because of how I was brought up and the prayers of my mother and father, I felt that I wanted to stay in their prayers. For example, even in my senior year of high school, when they allowed and encouraged me to make my own decisions, I would ask my parents for their advice. They would encourage me to pray about the decisions. I always felt that I knew where my parents stood regarding events, and I on my own decided to respect what I believed were their opinions. This is why it was such a struggle when I started to learn new truth. The main struggles were hellfire, the Sabbath, the condemnation for assurance of salvation, and the state of the dead.

We lost so many relatives at such a young age; funerals were always hard to understand. The minister would say that they were going straight to Heaven. Then, when we would get to the cemetery, they would be put in the ground, and the minister would say that this "Mortal must put on immortality at the resurrection." I knew that I Thessalonians 4:16 said, "The death in Christ shall rise first," and it seemed so inconsistent with what I heard at the funeral service. This would bother me so much: the inconsistency of where the person was when they died. When I would mention anything about this, others would say, "Oh, you just let this bother you too much."

Over time, I began a desperate deep struggle; it grew worse after hearing sermons and especially after evangelistic meetings in the UB Church. The minister would passionately proclaim, "Don't you leave this place tonight, you need to know beyond a shadow of a doubt that you are saved because you could end up in a car accident on the way home and you could go to hell and burn forever and ever!" After I heard this belief over and over, it frightened me, but I kept it hidden until I became very close to a complete nervous breakdown. Everyone shamed me for doubting the assurance of my salvation, including my own pastor. I always felt like there was some special moment or experience I had missed because although I have given my life to Jesus and believed I was "saved," I still felt there was something missing.

Finally, in desperation I pleaded with God to clarify this in a way I could understand, or let me die. In deep pain of heart, I was desperate for answers for why I couldn't gain peace of heart and why it was not coming together for me! So, I cried out, "Please God, help me to understand and find peace of mind or just let me die!" Then I heard a voice, it was not audible, but very much a voice, "Just die out to Me, and I'll show you. Give it all to Me, and I will show you." I remember calling the pastor to our house and saying to him that I heard God's voice in a way I had never heard before and I knew something was coming, but I didn't know what. To this, my minster said that I needed to see a doctor because he felt I was having a nervous breakdown and needed to get some help.

Soon I scheduled an appointment with Dr. Matthews, and explained what I was going through. What he said to me was, "Donna, you are perfectly healthy. You are having a spiritual battle, not a physical one. I would like you to visit my wife Betty, and tell her your story." I went home and pondered that for a couple of weeks, until one afternoon I just decided to put my young children in the car and go for a ride. I believe God urged me to do what came next, because I started up the road to that beautiful house that set up on a hill and drove up the long driveway to that home. As I approached the house on the side towards the garage, lo and behold Mrs. Matthews stood outside of the garage and came up to my window quickly. I rolled it down and she said, "You are Donna Clements, aren't you!?" I believe that God sent me because she had never met me or knew my car. Next, she said, "Come on in, I see you have your children with you. I will have my children watch yours, and I want to hear your story! My husband told me about you." So, I sat in the living room and explained the struggle that I had been going through and that her husband said that I should visit her and share my testimony. As we started to talk, I explained the struggle that I was in and how God had said He would make it clear to me. I started crying, and Betty then said, "Why don't you go into the front room for a few moments of quiet time." I remember it was a beautiful, large room with a fireplace. She encouraged me to spend some time alone praying and that she would be in the other room praying as well. I had said to her that this has been such a tremendous struggle, and I wasn't sure how to tell my family.

The Matthews Family

Then she said, "I would really like you to meet our pastor, Elder Roy Lemon." She said that he would come visit me and that I should tell him my story. I told her that I would accept that and so she had him come to our house. I still remember Elder Lemon asking if he could do Bible studies with me. He said, "Now, Donna, you will have to make your decision by faith and we will be there to support you." So, I decided to take Bible studies from Pastor Lemon, and everything I learned I knew was truth. There was a peace that came over me. Without a shadow of a doubt, God had answered my prayers because I had asked Him to show me or let me die. He was very clear in showing me the truth. I was ready. I wanted someone to study the Bible with and I thought this was terrific! No one had ever asked me about taking Bible studies. Before this, I always knew that my father was a real student of the Bible. He would talk with us so much about the things of the Bible; he knew so much. However, when I read, there were things that was hard for me to interpret or understand, and secretly I always wanted someone to help me understand. The hunger was there. I would read here or there, but I didn't know how to put it all together in a way that I knew that I needed. So, I thought this idea of taking Bible Studies was wonderful because it would help me to understand how everything connected together. When I did learn what the Bible said, I was amazed. After I had gone through studies with Elder Lemon, for the first time in my life, I felt like I knew what I believed because now it was clear to me!

When Elder Lemon asked me about being baptized, I wasn't sure what to do because I had already been Biblically baptized in the UB church. He said I didn't have to get rebaptized by immersion, and only needed to do confession of faith. But because my struggle was so deep and because I felt so deeply convinced that this was truth, I had the desire to be re-baptized. I had never had an experience like that in my life; I was compelled that it warranted being rebaptized.

When I first met Elder Lemon, I had no intention of changing churches; this didn't even come to my mind. I just truly wanted to understand, and have a better clarity of the Bible. After our studies when he asked, "Donna, now what are you going to do with it?" I thought, "What do you mean, what am I doing to do with it!?" When he made it clear enough that when someone accepts the truth, they need to do something about it, it hit me like a bolt of lightning. I only thought that I was looking for truth and how it fits together because I couldn't understand the inconsistencies. I didn't ever consider, until this point, that I was going to be making a change to another church! So, I told him that I needed to pray about it and that I would like all his church to be praying and soon it became clear to me that God was calling me to the Seventh-day Adventist Church.

The peace that came over me was incredible, but fear also set in because I realized that I would need to share with my family, and that my family could be torn apart over these changes that I was making. I mentioned my fear of telling my husband and how it could end our marriage. I shared that I wasn't sure how Harold would take it, but that if the church was praying along with me, I knew God would get us through it. I was also concerned because my Grandfather was a UB minister and that would affect everyone in the family, if they found out. I was concerned that Harold would leave me if I went through with this decision. But I knew that if God had brought me this far, I could trust Him by faith to continue to lead me through the next steps. I experienced peace like I had never had before; I knew that God was in it all. I simply do not know how to explain it, it was a peace that I never had even though I was already a Christian. You can't ask for truth and do nothing with it.

At this point, two or three of the major struggles had been answered in my mind, but these didn't necessarily change my lifestyle. However, the Sabbath issue was a hurdle that needed to be cleared because it would really change my interaction, especially with my husband and parents. When I told Harold, he was upset, but he allowed me to follow the convictions of my heart. He went to church on Sunday and I and the kids went to church on Sabbath. I told him he could also take the kids to church on Sunday if he wanted to. He said, "No, I don't want them to be confused. You take them with you." Harold felt that they would be better taught at the Adventist church. Our children loved the Sabbath school programs at the SDA church!

My parents had a large business at the farmers market in Lansing, Michigan, three days a week. As the business grew, they needed more help and as a teen I was asked to come with them to wait on the ever-growing customers. I was chosen to be the one to come to help because I liked meeting and interacting with other people. There was one problem, it meant that I had to rise early (I was not an early morning person)! I often drove my mom to the market when Dad was working on the farm either harvesting or planting crops. I struggled to quickly make change for customers; my parents said I had to count backwards. It was so confusing, but I learned how. So now, my desperate worry was how to tell my parents, who I helped at the Farmers' Market every Saturday that I could not help them any longer, because of my commitment and my new found solid faith in the Sabbath. I had told the church that it was important that they needed to be praying because I knew that this was going to be a big one and that without much prayer, I would not be able to get through it. Although I know it hurt my parents, I think the Good Lord helped them to see and accepted my change better than I even expected.

Even my father had talked about the Ten Commandments. So, when the Sabbath topic came up, I remembered that he had told us children that the Catholic church had changed the Sabbath from Saturday to Sunday (though they had no right to, and my dad didn't even believe that they had that right). My father was an extremely strong person on the Ten Commandments. However, he believed that the *tradition* of Christ's Resurrection on the first day of the week justified the change and kept him firm on Sunday worship. So, when he questioned me later about this topic, I reminded him of all the things he told us, and that I had found a church that believed that the Sabbath had never been changed. I could not find anything in the teaching of the United Brethren church, or by him or my grandfather, that could change the Sabbath day. When I explained this to him, although he was still somewhat upset, he now had been lovingly cornered by his own words. I reminded my father, as he had reminded us, that the Ten Commandments, written by God Himself, were many times confused by protestant churches with the ceremonial law. My personal testimony to my father was that he himself had taught us that the Law had never been done away with. I told him, "God made it very clear in my struggle that you were right, Dad: the Sabbath was *not* done away with because it is in the Ten Commandants, written by God." After that, my dad never said another word about it to me.

I was baptized on May 15, 1965, by Pastor Roy Lemon. The support I received from my new church family was amazing, including Esther Helton, Marilyn Fox, Dr. Sevener, and the Matthews family. They launched into helping me more than anyone I had ever met; I called it nurturing. The people were so sincere and supportive when I started attending the church. The church really rallied around me. This is something that we cannot allow to be lost in our churches today; we often allow people to slip away because we do not give them the support they need.

I still remember my very first visit to the Adventist church. Dr. Sevener was greeting that day and walked right up to me and gave such a welcome that you knew he was sincere and very joyful. I never forgot that. My point here is that we really need to be aware of this in our churches today. I don't think that people feel the support that I did that day. We see too many go back out, even baptized people, and we wonder, "What happened? What went wrong?" We need to nurture.

Soon after I was baptized, the church began to talk with me about how my children should be in the church school. I agreed! Then I started to struggle again... *How in the world would I tell Harold that I would like to have the children in the church school!?* So, I asked the church, "Before I approach him, I need to know that everyone in the church will be praying, because this is a serious matter!" After they all promised that they would be in prayer, I let them know when I was going to approach him. I did so in faith because I understood that we did not have the finances to just start paying tuition. I said, "Lord, I'm going to trust You. I'm doing this in totally blind faith." His reaction was pretty much what I thought it would be. He said, "No way on earth can we afford to pay for tuition!" I thought it was final, but it was not final in God's eyes or in Harold's, even though, I didn't know at the time. Shortly after, Harold approached me and asked, "Do you still want our kids in the church school?" I answered, "Very much so." He said, "I think I've got an idea. If you and your church really believe what you say (towards Christian education), then you tell the church to be praying, and you pray and I'll be praying. I'll approach my boss man and see what he has to say." Harold explained to his boss that he could make door hinges for less than the current purchase price. He also knew it meant borrowing some money to purchase the equipment and tables to set up in the basement. Dick Trumley said, "What are you waiting for? Get busy!" The kids were excited! They had made friends and absolutely wanted to be in that church school. Their reaction affected both Harold and me and it would be better than public school; so, prayers were answered. The three older children, Steven, Scott, and Sim immediately started in the SDA school system. Mike, our youngest son, had to go to the public kindergarten because the SDA school didn't have a Kindergarten program, at that time. It was obvious he was extremely unhappy. He didn't say anything, but was very solemn. Soon, I found out the real reason was because he missed his brothers and wanted to be in the SDA school with them. The school and the teacher agreed to allow him to come to the

SDA school even though they did not officially have a kindergarten program. From then on, everything went fine. All our children went through our church school, and grew up in the Seventh-day Adventist faith. Harold was still attending the UB church, up until our children were grown and had their own children.

In the spring of 2009, our church was having an upcoming evangelistic meeting, and I invited Harold to join me. I think Sim had some part in getting him to attend as well. Harold attended most every meeting, and at the end they had a call for decisions and all of a sudden, he walked out of his seat and towards the front and I just sat there in total shock until Simeon came up to me and said, "Mother, aren't you going to join Dad and support him?" So, then I went up there. It made a big difference in our family that we were all united in the same faith and church.

In closing, allow me to re-emphasize the struggles and pain I felt were abundantly real. Yet, looking back, I need to acknowledge that Jesus was directing us, one step at a time. Each time I look back, I am still amazed by how the Lord has led. The oneness that we now feel as a family is only partially because of us, but mostly because of Jesus. I cannot help but say, praise the Lord! He is still in control.

Chapter Twenty-seven

HAROLD'S STEADY CHURCH TRANSITION

Someone has said, "The only thing in life that is constant, is change." While others may say, "The more they change, the more they stay the same." There, of course, is an element of truth and error in both approaches.

Each of us handle change differently. It can be slow, methodical, spontaneous, or planned; but, sooner or later, an element called *tradition* will have to be reckoned with. Most of us won't even acknowledge the hold it has on our life. For instance, if your father, mother, grandfather, grandmother are from a certain political party, there is a good chance it is your party also. Again, if the majority of your folks, through two or more generations, went to a certain denomination, or church, you probably will also. If the belief in that church is solid and constant in a given area, your thinking also will follow that line. With all the above being true, we will also need to admit that my personal thoughts and feelings will play a deep essential part.

My wife and I both came from the same church background, the United Brethren in Christ. Her grandfather, Rev. J. I. Batdorff, as mentioned earlier, was not only a minister, but a superintendent in the denomination. Her uncle also was a minister in our church. My brother, Darrell, and Donnie's brother-in-law Wayne, both preached in our church, at least part-time, and in other strong fundamental churches.

Although Donnie and I differed in the depth of our feelings and the problems we faced, there are a couple of areas that bothered us equally. When funerals were held for loved ones, friends and others, the officiating minister would make a pulpit remark indicating that the deceased individual was already up in Heaven, enjoying the beauties of the New Jerusalem with Jesus. Shortly thereafter, we would meet at the graveside service and the minister would be quoting I Thessalonians 4:13-17. Verse 17 is very clear that when Jesus returns in the clouds with a shout, those sleeping in Jesus (the dead in Christ) will rise from the grave first, and then we which are alive and remain will be caught up together with the Lord, and ascend into Heaven. These two concepts just don't match! For Donnie and I, at least, this tradition or thinking needed to be changed in our lives.

Let's step back for a moment and reconsider what was written in the early chapters of Acts. After His resurrection, Jesus walked and talked with His disciples for 40 days, as mentioned in Acts 1:3. There Jesus promised that the Holy Spirit would replace Him after His ascension and the disciples would be baptized with the Holy Spirit at that time. In Acts chapter one, Jesus was taken up in a cloud and two angels clearly stated that this *same* Jesus, in like manner, will return someday. We have been looking for Him to fulfill that promise through most of our lives. Allow me to throw in one note that I find interesting. While teaching the adult Sunday school class in the UB church, my uncle (one of my mother's brothers) made the statement that he had heard that Jesus was going to return ever since he was a kid, and that was 60 years ago. The indication was, "I've heard this so long, I'm not sure when the *now* is going to be." I paused for a moment and then said to my uncle, "All you have told me is that His coming is 60 years closer now than it was then. We need to be ready." Now back to the story.

I want to re-emphasize the statement, *"This same Jesus."* Throughout our lives, we have seen a thousand things that have been used as a substitute for the real thing. For instance, butter is now margarine, and you can fill in the nine hundred other things. But let me be clear. For *Jesus there isn't any substitute*! He Himself said, "I will return!" And then in Revelation 22:12, He stated, "Behold, I come quickly." Let's not concentrate on the time, let's concentrate every morning that *this* could be the day. Now let's restate that those two thoughts at the pulpit, and later at the graveside, don't line up. The first says that they are in Heaven; the second says they are sleeping in the grave. One of the two cannot be right! Allow me to give an illustration: when Jesus died on that center cross, one of the thieves said, "Lord, remember me when You come into Your Kingdom." Jesus said, "I say to you today that you will be with me in paradise." But where did they both go that day? They both went to the grave. If the statement was taken at face value, instead of singing, "Up from the grave He arose" on resurrection morning (Sunday), you would have to sing, "Back from Heaven He came!" All serious Bible scholars acknowledge that the punctuation in Greek, Aramaic, and Hebrew, was different in that day than what would be used today. When Jesus made this statement, He did not mean you will be in paradise today, meaning *right now*. It simply meant I say to you today (comma!), you will be with me in paradise. I suppose we need to make clear one thought: the Bible says the *dead are dead*. We are not just some *beings,* flowing hither and yon, here, or there. If we are not careful, this is where spiritualism comes in.

With that cleared up, for both Donnie and I, one of the other issues is the fourth commandment which is on the Sabbath day. When God went through the work that He did, in the six days of creation, He Himself rested on the Seventh Day. Many times, there appears to be confusion with most churches and ministers in the difference between the ceremonial law versus God's Ten Commandments which was written by the finger of God etched in stone. There are only eight times in the New Testament where the first day of the week (Sunday) is mentioned. Five of them directly relate to His resurrection, but none of the eight say, "change the day." At the same time, there are hundreds of places in the Old and New Testament that refer to the fourth commandment, which is the only commandment that says, *"Remember."*

If you ask any firm, Bible-based preaching/teaching minister, they would all say that Jesus is not only our Lord and Savior, our Friend, and our soon coming King, but also our example in all things. Guess what day He worshipped on? The New Testament is abundantly clear that as His custom was, He would be found in the synagogue, temple, or place of worship on the Seventh day. As a side note, if you go later to the New Testament, even Paul, in his writing, was teaching on the Sabbath day, in some cases three or four Sabbaths in a row expounding the Word. This was clearly well after the resurrection.

So, allow me to be clear of my understanding at this point. All ministers know that Jesus clearly worshiped on the Sabbath, then in I Peter 2:17 we find the words that Jesus left us an example that we should follow in His steps. So, if Jesus is our leader, which He is, and if He kept the Sabbath day, which He did, and if we are to follow in His steps, as we should, then this illustration is clear. If the Sabbath is good enough for Jesus, it is good enough for me. Case closed.

No Adventist, or otherwise, has ever been stronger on Christian education than myself. Back when I was in school, the late 40s, Bible was a legitimate course, still offered by most Michigan schools. Our teacher, Mrs. Kiplinger, was excellent in my opinion in presenting the Bible as a strong historical book, covering the main topics without getting into the side eddies of any particular church's pet peeve. But guess what? Even though the founding fathers wanted us to keep God as our leader, we have successfully removed God and Christian education from our public-school system. Shame on us. I believe that my generation in the 50s and 60s were the last that were allowed these essential courses. Therefore, when my good wife Donnie indicated my resistance to Christian education, it only had reference to one area. I was all for putting the children into a Christian school, but I am a very firm believer that any Christian individual should not rely just on other people or the church to educate their child. I have personally seen too many times when it was made so easy for the children and parents, that as soon as the educational process was completed, they drifted away because they did not have their heart and soul into the education, including their own personal finances. So, when Donnie asked me about schooling, it had nothing to do with anything but finances. With a family of seven, how could I afford to put the five children in Christian school? I do not believe we gain a whole lot by putting our hands out to accept everything from everyone else. We made certain the children understood that if and when we made the decision, they would have to make financial commitments of extra work just as I had to add a couple of odd jobs. In other words, roll up your sleeves and go to work, or just don't do it.

Allow me to point out that in my major job with Carefree, I was director of purchasing at that time. I was buying hinges for aluminum storm doors from a company out of Lowell, Michigan. At one time they raised us 20 percent which was more than our company could afford. The light bulb went on. Although I had a boss that was strong in his verbiage using terms and words I would never think of using, he still appeared to have respect for me. So, at noon one day I told my wife, "You pray hard, I'm going to attempt to solve our problem."

After much prayer, I went into the boss's office and closed the door. I told him, "Dick, what would happen if I would borrow the money for several OBI presses, and manufacture the hinges for our company at the *old price?* If I can do this, there is only one problem: there is a key conflict of interest because of my title." Without any of his usual unpleasant verbiage, he said, "What's your problem? You've got a good secretary, let her bring all the parts and keep a separate file on the inbound parts and all the completed hinges sold back to the company. If there is a difference in count, obviously, you would owe that to the company, therefore making the project legitimate. What's your problem? Go for it!" I about fainted, but I immediately went to an individual in the SDA congregation, told him how much money I would need to buy the presses, how I planned to put them all in our damp Michigan cellar, complete the hinges, and sell them back to the company. I told him what the figure was, and that if he would grant it, I think I could have him paid back in one year. He gave me the money on the spot, did not charge me any interest and we had the project paid for in nine months. It is safe to say that the Clements family produced in their basement, in excess of five million hinges!

For the record, there are three leaves to the hinge, the large center section goes on the back edge of the door, the two smaller end sections go to the z-bar that goes around the door. These were put together with a 3/16 aluminum pin that we also had to buy, cut the side, along with punching the hinge parts. It was assembled with two bronze washers, separating the three aluminum parts. There was other work that needed to be done, but basically there were weeks that we would manufacture 10,000 hinges per week, many times it would be up to 14,000 to 16,000 per week.

As you can see, this took a lot of extra labor on my part, because I would have to carry all the heavy parts up and down the stairs, as well as run the last press which secured the hinge parts in place. We paid our children, other Adventist children who needed money, and neighborhood kids to keep us going. If you seriously ask God to help you, this just proves that where there is a will, there *is* a way.

One other area that needs to be clarified is that where my wife had a very difficult time struggling with her spiritual problems, mine, by comparison, were more slow and deliberate without the extreme tension that she had. Allow me to clear up one other area: when she informed me that she wanted the children to go to church with her, I made the hardest decision of my life. I did not want to see our children become a spiritual pawn. I did not want to allow them to go with her on Sabbath, and then to be *fair* go with me on Sunday. This I knew would be very confusing to them in their young minds, and I absolutely could not allow it to happen.

I had a discussion with my wife, also related to tithe and offerings. I could have just taken most of it to my church and let her worry about her end, but I thought the only fair thing to do was to split the tithe and offerings equally to both churches, which we did. I have never regretted the decision that we made.

Now with the children going to the SDA Sabbath school and church, that left me for approximately 15 years to go to my church alone. Again, not an easy decision. During this time, I was so much for Christian education, and the singing of our family, that we were all the time becoming more involved in the Seventh-day Adventist church and doctrine so my transition was slower and more methodical than my wife's. Mine was simply, "Okay, when do I make the change?" My not telling this to my wife, you can understand her surprise when at one of the meetings held at the Charlotte Church (and in fact at the school), I told Elder Jim Micheff that I would be coming forward at the end of the meeting. As a side note, as I went forward, Sim our son said, "Mother, aren't you going up with Dad?" My not telling her ahead of time, she was shocked when I went forward.

In closing, for my UB family (which I had been a part of for well over 100 years, when you consider my parents, and grandparents) it was hard for them to understand my move, as they even questioned my faith as a father as to what I was doing with my children. After all, I had taught Sunday school for roughly 50 years and was Sunday School Superintendent. I led the singing, sang in church, did solo work, so they were all saying, *"Why?"* The bottom line is that it was a tough decision. Making the move that I had to make for both me and my family, there is no question that it strengthened my faith, my love for Jesus, and the church.

Though I had been baptized in Sebewa Creek at roughly 12 years old, I still felt it was important not only for my faith but for the faith of some others at the time that my going into baptism would encourage them. So, in November of 2009, I was re-baptized.

The old saying is, "All is well that ends well." For the family to now be one under Christ and the church as a unit had now been satisfied. There was now no longer any question about who was right, or who was wrong. Jesus had led both my wife and I differently, but the end result was the same. The oneness that we can now experience as a family was worth all the struggle, for both of us.

Chapter Twenty-eight

THE DAY THE SUN
ROSE IN THE WEST

Oops! Here we are, the book is nearly completed and I haven't revealed to you yet where the book title came from. I guess it's about time! I indicated earlier that I was very involved in helping set up the National Window Standards in accordance with the American Architectural Manufacturing Association (AAMA) for prime window companies that involved all different types of structures. The frames could be vinyl, wood, aluminum, steel, or composite (a combination of two different materials).

I can say that, for the most part, while determining the window standards, the engineers, general managers, vice presidents, presidents, and other representatives of the companies honestly tried to work hard to find a solution, as long as it didn't hurt their company. Finding neutral ground was hard to come by, but appeared to be in our reach. That particular day was a typical day at Carefree. I worked hard in the morning to get my work caught up, dashed to the Lansing, Michigan airport (about 25 miles away), and caught a flight headed to St. Louis, Missouri, which was the connecting flight to San Jose, California.

Just my luck, so to speak, the flight was running at least 20 minutes behind as we were headed to Lambert Field Airport. The time of year would have been late June or early July (the longest days of the year). The year would have been between 1978 and 1981. The airport was between 450-500 feet above sea level. Running through the airport I had called ahead to see if they could hold the fight for approximately ten minutes. In those days, many times at least in good weather, you would load up on the tarmac and would simply run up the stairs into the plane. Being in pretty good shape, although it was hot, I actually sprinted between a quarter and half a mile to get to the plane. At the top of the stairs, I looked to the west and the sun had *fully set* with only a reflection in the sky. I went to my seat quickly and they had waited long enough that before I had gotten my seat belt fastened and adjusted, they had already gotten the stairs rolled away and the airplane door shut. Though it has been years I think the plane was either a 720 or one of the earlier versions of a 737.

Within a minute or two, we were rolling down the runway ready for take-off. I had never before seen a take-off that quick from my entering the plane. We immediately lifted off and started our fast climb to a higher altitude which was approximately 36,000 feet. All but immediately the sun started to re-appear in the western sky. The speed of the sun coming up was almost startling. Oh yes, I know, it is the earth's rotation and not the sun actually rising, but we all know that. This sounds dumb, but if I could have reached out the window with an overgrown tape measure the distance between the earth, and the *bottom* of the sun, appeared to be about 20 feet. At this time, we had reached our cruising altitude and the pilot came on to say that we were now doing 575 mph. Remember we had already gone through the eastern time zone to central time zone, and shortly after we left St. Louis, we would be crossing into mountain time zone. Of course, our final time zone would be the Pacific time zone, as we approached California.

I checked with a friend of mine who is involved with flying and he indicated that what I was thinking was correct. A: the altitude of 36,000 feet would explain why the sun was now showing as high in the sky as it was; and B: because of the speed, as indicated 575 mph, nearly neutralized the moving from time zone to time zone and would explain why the sun *appeared* to almost permanently stand still in the sky. In the two and a half to three hours that it took us to fly to California, two of the hours were still showing the sun in the same basic location. This reminds me of the time in the Bible when it talked about how sun stood still, Joshua 10:13,14.

I admit that this appearance of the stillness of the sun caused me to have great peace and struck with a feeling of awe. It was as if Jesus had pulled back the curtain on the stage of life, and I'm just simple enough to believe He did it just for me. There are no words to describe that absolute peace. This rotation of the earth appeared to be in perfect sync and harmony just to emphasize the moment. No wonder God's Word says in Psalms 46:10, "Be still and *know* that I am God." What an awesome God we serve.

Frankly, it was not until the last 45 minutes of the flight that the sun (the second time of the day for me) was setting. That deep peace and comfort for those two hours was something that I have never been able to erase from my mind. The chorus of Wonderful Peace written by W. G. Cooper goes as follows,

> Peace! Peace! Wonderful peace
> Coming down from the Father above
> Sweep over my spirit forever I pray
> In fathomless billows of love

The next morning, I did get to our AAMA meeting on time, and the return flight back to Michigan the following morning was back to normal with no significant problems. Even today, I still cannot wrap my mind around how incredible that moment was and that He did it especially for me.

As Christians, many times we come to the parting of life where a mother, father, sibling, mate, son, daughter, or close friend has passed away, and we just don't quite know how to say goodbye at that moment. One morning, like 4 a.m., it finally struck me. When Jesus ascended, the angels said in the book of Acts, "Why do you stand gazing up into heaven? This same Jesus who was taken up from you into heaven, will so come in like manner as you saw Him go." There is no substitute here. Jesus is the One and Only Savior of the world. In essence, He was saying, "I shall return!" Here is the poem from that early morning:

So Long for Now
(This poem was written early Sabbath morning,
April 22, 2017, by Harold Clements)

After Jesus rose triumphantly
On that great resurrection day;
He walked and talked with His disciplines
About 40 days or so they say.

He told them He would send His Spirit
Before (or as) He did depart
The Spirit would be their comforter
As He entered into their heart.

In Acts we are told He ascended
As He was taken up that day;
When He left, He said he would return
To take them Home to stay.

So friends we must be ready
With our lamps all trimmed and bright
Waiting for His soon return
When He makes all things right.

The day will soon come, when we depart
Though we don't know when or how;
We won't need to say "Goodbye"
It's just "So long, (salute) for now!"

I will close this book by just saying, "So long for now," because
we will meet again.

In Christian Love,
Harold Clements

About the Author

The author, Harold Clements, is eighty-eight years old and has wanted to write this book for the last forty years. He is a Christian husband, married sixty-five years to the love of his life, a father (dad) of five, grandfather of fourteen, and great-grandfather of six (so far!). Born to a Christian family, there has always been singing in his family, his wife's family, their children, grandchildren, and great-grandchildren's lives. The author has a sense of humor, stories of answers to prayer, and near-death experiences. The experiences of his father and his span nearly a century of farming (the twentieth-century). The author feels fortunate that he lived in a century where he could still experience the "American Dream" because he started working in the small plant of Carefree, with only seven employees, worked his way up to director of purchasing, helped the company grow to over 500 employees, and was general manager for over fifteen years before his retirement. Also, upon so-called retirement, he sold and installed thousands of vinyl replacement windows. The author helped set the National Window Standards for vinyl windows and all styles of windows. The author, always active in sports and healthy eating habits has helped keep this old man alive and well. For instance, after retiring, he joined the Polk County Senior Olympics and competed in the 50 and 100-meter dashes between the ages of 65-77. The author, from the "old-school" way of life, is still proudly representing Jesus, the American flag, God, and country.

Ingram Content Group UK Ltd.
Milton Keynes UK
UKHW012052190423
420461UK00013B/246/J